Through These Eyes

Surrendering the Ties of My Soul

Written by Yladrea Drummond

Through These Eyes

Copyright © Yladrea Drummond, 2020

Cover image: © Chocolate Readings

ISBN-13: 978-0-578-74331-8

Publisher's Note

Printed and bound in the United States of America. All rights reserved. No part of this book may be reproduced or transmitted in any form or by any means, electronic or mechanical, including photocopying, recording, or by any information storage and retrieval system except by a review who may quote brief passages in a review to be printed in a magazine, newspaper, or on the Web without permission in writing from Yladrea Drummond.

Although the author and publisher have made every effort to ensure the accuracy and completeness of information contained in this book, we assume no responsibility for errors, inaccuracies, omissions, or any inconsistency herein. The storyline, advice and strategies contained herein may not be suitable for your situation. Neither the publisher nor the author shall be liable for damages arising here from.

Dedication

To everything that tried to hold me back and everything that set me free.

Through These Eyes

Contents

Introduction — 7

Chapter 1
Beautifully Scarred — 15

Chapter 2
Let's Not Confuse the Facts — 37

Chapter 3
Delayed Not Denied — 55

Chapter 4
Forgive Yourself — 77

Chapter 5
Highest In The Room — 96

Chapter 6
Silence Speaks Volumes — 115

Chapter 7
A Moment Like This — 127

Acknowledgements — *133*
Meet Yladrea — *134*

Through These Eyes

Introduction

"I am in charge of my journey - I give myself permission to start over as many times as I need to."

Mood
Ways - Jhené Aiko

First things first, we all are a "somebody" in at least one portion of this world. But to you, I'm likely a nobody. AND THAT'S FINEEEEEE! But like my girl, Phaedra Parks said, during the greatest read of all time, "But what you will know" is that by the end of this book, you will at least know my story. Truthfully, I've thought of this moment, me sitting here writing about my life for you all to read for years. Specifically, I knew I would write a book about how unbelievably FUCKED up my life was. I would say to myself, People won't believe this shit, but they need to hear it. Every year the thought to write would cross my mind. I'd put it as one of my New Year's Resolutions, and every year no book was written. I never stopped to ask myself why I never checked that off my list. See, what you will soon learn about me is that I'm a glorified procrastinator, with a ton of excuses, I'm impulsive and indecisive all at the same time. I have a freakishly good memory, and I'm a person that accomplishes almost all of my goals at all costs.

Yep, you guessed it, I'm a Libra.

Anyway, I shared that with you to show you that, me not ever fulfilling the goal of writing this book, was not the norm of my character. But here we are eleven years removed from the original thought of this book, and I've finally recognized what took me so long.

Over those past eleven years, I was completely lost.

Wait a minute. Let me start over. Hell, if I'm going to do this right, I have to keep it all the way real with myself consciously.

Okay, boom, for the past eighteen years, if I'm being exact, I was entirely lost. So, let's see, that means from my eleventh birthday, all the way until the month after I turned twenty-nine this past year, I had no sense of self, like AT ALL. I used to say it felt like a bad dream, but it was more than a dream, it was real, and I lived through it. More specifically, what I was experiencing were years of being hostage to Soul Ties.

Now look, I lie to you not, I had no idea what the heck a soul tie was until I turned twenty-nine. It wasn't until after I had already released myself from those soul ties that I even knew that's what they were. I knew what I encountered was evil, abnormal, and downright toxic. But it was more than that. A soul tie is said to form after an intensely close spiritual or emotional relationship. Soul ties make you feel like you are suffocating like you are about to drown. They make you feel like you can't shake the funk or that there is no way out. Well, that's at least how they made me feel. And since this is my book, my story, and my truth, that's what we are going to call them today.

Anyways, getting back to us getting acquainted.

I'm sure we've all heard stories of children who grew up in toxic households, endured abuse and lost their way. They inherit many toxic familial norms, behaviors, and habits. These inherited traits take hostage of their mind, constricts how they process situations, and influences how they transition through life. While not every child fits that narrative, a significant number will identify with its core message.

Unfortunately, half fall victim to their circumstances, and as they become adults, they fail to thrive. That half is what society likes to call a "Product of Their Environment," as they shake their head in disappointment. The other half are those that become adults and learn the art of faking it 'til they make it. They learn to separate their misery from the life they think they deserve. To the public eye, this half looks well put together and accomplished. But behind the scenes, they are swirling through life, being self-destructive like a tornado, with no means or sight of better days. That half are those that I like to call, the "Perpetrators."

I guess by now you can guess which half of the spectrum I fell. It's hard to imagine that I was that girl.

No, for real, I get pissed every time I think about who I used to be and where it all started. I get mad that reflecting makes me mad. As I see it, anger is sometimes the necessary tool to overcome the shitty times. Quite frankly, it was anger that caused my breakthrough.

And music.

Music is a powerful thing. Music will have you thinking you can conquer the world with one song. I deliberately made playlists based on my mood. Seriously, I even have a playlist named PISSED. I ain't shame!

I mean, I know for sure I can't be the only person who listens to a song and thinks it's written just for me. I mean, like really embody the whole persona of the song. The kind where you are at the red light screaming every word at the top of your lungs, and you look to your right only to see the person in the other car next to you giggling while mouthing the words, "she feeling it." Yep, I am that girl. And while that moment may be the truest to self that I used to get, it was also scary.

Music was dangerous for a person like me. I allowed so many songs to be the solution or the way I solved many issues.

Process what I just said.

I let songs dictate the fate of my life. Wow. Just typing that right now gave me chills. Admitting that you didn't have a mind of your own is not easy. But that simply is what it is.

The statement, "I survived," makes me cringe. Not because it isn't a valid statement, because it most definitely is valid. I cringe because I must've said it a thousand times as a way to make myself think I had moved past situations. But guess what...your girl was LYING. I later realized I hadn't survived anything; I just learned to create delusions to make it easier for me to "adjust." Let's be very clear; adjusting is not surviving. A person who survives, at minimum, chooses to continue to live unbothered after a shitty moment. I wasn't a survivor, and I damn sure was one hundred percent BOTHERED.

During our time together, I want you all to hold me accountable for the words in these chapters. From this sentence forward, I promise I won't sugar coat my truth. On this journey, I'll share my unfiltered thoughts, the experiences that held me hostage, and, most importantly, the moment that set me free. So, I want you to grab your wine, get comfortable, and go to the place that relaxes you most. If you are anything like me, a person that embodies the emotional moments of others, even when watching a comedy movie, then this will be your newest emotional rollercoaster. Like all rollercoasters, this book will have its share of highs and lows. I don't know about you, but every time I took my seat on a ride, I'd damn near be in tears as they came around to make sure we were securely strapped in.

The rollercoaster ride would take off and begin its cliché slow creep upward, building suspense before the big drop. Of course, me being me, I would start whining to the person next to me, pleading for the ride to be over before it truly began. Seriously, I would do the absolute most. But when the short adventure was over, you would've thought I was someone else, the way I'd strut off that ride like I had conquered the world.

I never forgot the emotions that I felt when I rode a rollercoaster. I also never forgot a single feeling I felt as I journeyed to self-healing. I hope you never forget your emotions too.

I hope that through the highs and lows of this book, you allow yourself to feel, face your fears, open your thoughts, and if I get lucky, you may even let some of what I share help you start to heal.

So here we go! Take a look through these eyes. I welcome you to enter my world. This is how I surrendered the ties of my soul.

I. Acceptance

Chapter 1
Beautifully Scarred
Sometimes your heart needs more time to accept what your mind already knows.

Mood

Forever Don't Last - Jazmine Sullivan
Wrong Side of a Love Song - Melanie Fiona
Used to Love U - John Legend

Have you ever used a word in a sentence solely because you know that it fits in that particular space? But when you sit back and ask yourself what the word means, you realize you don't honestly know its exact definition. You just use it out of habit. Then in one random moment of curiosity, you go look it up to confirm or clarify your assumed meaning of that word. Only to find out that you only scratched the surface of its denotation. But now that you know its full definition, it makes everything crystal clear. I like to call that the "ah-ha" moment. And while we all wish those moments occur early on, it doesn't take away the effect they have whenever it does finally happen.

I remember having a conversation about messed up relationships, with a former coworker, during our business trip in New Hampshire. She mentioned how her ex-partner was a narcissist and how that person truly messed with her mind. She asked me had I ever dealt with a narcissist before.

Instantly, I paused, trying to think of any encounter that I may have had with one when I realized that I don't honestly know. So, I said, "To tell you the truth, I don't know because while I have a general idea of what a narcissist is, I never took the time to actually look it up." Her response was something that will stand true until the end of time. She looked me dead in my eyes and said, "Look it up and after you do, believe me when you come across a narcissist, you won't question it, you will instantly notice them for who they are and their capabilities."

Chileeeeeee, I couldn't wait to get to my room to look it up. And my oh my, I was not prepared for what that definition revealed in my life, but I am forever grateful.

I know that some of ya'll don't know the characteristics of a narcissist. To save you some time in your research, just understand, a narcissist is like a tornado, they will destroy anyone and anything that crosses its path, while at the same time making you feel like it was your fault for not evacuating. When that tornado stops, it's gone, leaving everyone it hit to dwell on its damage and piece their lives back together. So, heed my warning, just like a tornado alert, when you encounter a narcissist… RUN FOR YOUR LIFE!!!!

Now that we've somewhat defined narcissism, I guess there is no reason to save the "best" for last.

Ya'll remember those soul ties I mentioned earlier? Well, welcome to my BIGGEST one.

When I was eleven, I found out that the man I grew to know as my dad, indeed, was not my dad. I was not switched at birth, nor adopted. As a matter of fact, my biological father is currently my legal stepfather. Yes, you read that right, I'll give you a minute to let that sink in… my "real" dad is the man my mom is married to. Just writing that right now had me feeling like I am in a scene of the Bold and Beautiful. Seriously, my life is a real-life soap opera. It's too muuuuuch. I get annoyed having to make it make sense to others. But in this instance, this information is vital for your understanding, so I'll give a quick level set.

The day I found out about my real dad, my life changed forever, I lost my childhood in that very moment. My real father told me the truth, and he became my "TRUTH TELLER." I had so many questions, and he had all the answers. I didn't realize how messed up that was for him to tell me that at such a young age. I mean, it really screwed me up.

You see, before that moment, my mom was perfect in my eyes; she literally could do no wrong. Then BOOM she wasn't perfect. She was a liar. It was like a switch went off in my head. I began to rebel and resent her. I was angry, and my actions reflected as such. But I never went to her about it. I just held it in.

Now let's be clear; my rebellion was subtle and weak. I would talk back or let my grades suffer. I began to entertain boys and drama at school. But nothing extreme. I just did enough to make sure my mom would notice. Well, as anticipated, she noticed. However, what I never accounted for was the change in her behavior. She began to show rage over minuscule things, from the way I combed my hair to the way I walked. Her demeanor towards me was aggressive and hostile as if I were her enemy. Crazy thing is, I don't think that she changed. I believe that as a child with a child's mentality, I was shielded from her actual character. But because the veil had been lifted so early, I had the ability to see the real her. She was no longer the superwoman I once knew her to be.

While I could see her through adult eyes, my mind still only had the capacity of a child. A child's mind is weak. A weak mind is a narcissist's biggest playground. If you haven't guessed it by now, my mom is a GRADE A narcissist. As a child, I was no match.

She groomed me. It's almost similar to how a predator lures in its victims. Predators will use a person's vulnerability to isolate them, make the person dependent on them, build an emotional relationship, and give them gifts/special privileges to gain trust. Let me set the record straight: my mom in no shape or form is a predator. Honestly, she was somewhat of a player if you ask me. But let's not get off-topic. I am merely giving you a depiction of the similarities in her tactics that she used to shape me as a person.

Imagine having a provider in your life that gave you everything you needed to survive. They allowed you to participate in all things constructive in your life and never missed a beat when it came to supporting by presence. Imagine that same provider making you believe they are the only person in your corner. Making you feel worthless when you don't follow their lead. Continuously, physically and mentally tearing you down at times when you were trying to grow. Stopping at nothing in their pursuit to tarnish your name and character to outsiders, to gain allies for future justification of their despicable behavior.

Do you feel confused yet? Conflicted even? That behavior is the perfect depiction of "you love me; you love me not." It's hard to imagine now and even harder to realize I lived it.

Let me break this down.

She isolated me. She rarely let me hang out with my friends. Being punished every weekend is an understatement. I often believe she separated me to make sure that no one else could speak positivity and life into me.

In the rare chance that I had the freedom to roam, she would coach me and my thoughts on what to share and what not to share. I became so good at only giving people parts of me, the parts that I wanted them to see. Truthfully, I should've been an actress.

In those times of isolation, she would always have these talks about everyone around me and their less than acceptable behavior. She would always tell me how much of a follower I was, and I needed to learn how to lead. I later realized she broke me down so much that I didn't have an identity of my own. So how could I ever lead if I was trained to follow? She made me think that my thoughts were so off base. And it didn't end once I became an adult, it only worsened.

Every time I dated someone, she would always nudge at the notion that I must be so insecure or think so low of myself that I would date a man who doesn't have the same views as her or my family. That is INSANE! She would always ask me what I did wrong if I told her that I stopped being friends with someone. In so many ways, she showed me how weak she thought I was and how little stock she had in me. "But she is your mom at the end of the day," is what people would say when I would tell them things about her. And those people were TRASH, and I should've left them there.

She made me dependent. But not on a man. She didn't teach me how to cook or show me an example of how to be a great wife. No, that wasn't her style. She always preached sustainability to me and never did that sermon include dependency on a man.

I remember, Webbie had just made a national anthem for women. He had us yelling I.N.D.E.P.E.N.D.E.N.T. at the top of our lungs. I think he met my mom in another lifetime because that song was her motto. But while most moms teach independence as a lifestyle, mine taught me it's okay never to need a man, but you will always need your mother. Now correct me if I am wrong, and maybe I am the only one misinformed. But as a Christian, I have never seen that in the bible. Never. Like ever.

I have to admit that all wasn't bad, though. Now and then, she gave me a glimmer of joy. As a child, she paid for me to play elite club volleyball. We would travel all the time. It was my escape and the one thing that allowed us to enjoy each other's company. Sometimes, I would forget how terrible she was because this escape filled so many voids.

As an adult, she began to treat me more like her friend and less like a little child at times. We would talk and laugh about adult topics until it didn't fit into a category that she wanted to discuss. If she saw that she was losing her grip, she would switch it up super quick. She would always put me in a "child's" place to remain superior.

She controlled me. It was subconscious more than conscious, almost like a trance. As a child, we didn't go to church. So, my faith lingered on her every word. For some time, I completely lost my faith in God. I mean, how could he leave me there with her.

Why didn't he save me from her command, mistreatment, and abuse? Through much prayer and pain, I realized he was there knowing that I could weather the storm.

I knew she was toxic, but my body still would allow her to push buttons and pull strings. My mind was tangled in her web. I wanted to be free, but I couldn't shake her, no matter how hard I thought I tried.

But one day, I simply woke up. It was like a thief in the night. I didn't see it coming. I won't complain because I am just glad the day came.

I'm genuinely sorry that cancer chose my mom. But what's worse is that she decided to use cancer as a tool for manipulation. Just when I thought I had seen the worst of her ways; she shows me an even uglier side to her. Ordinary people who receive a diagnosis of cancer tend to try to find peace for themselves; they try to live out their wildest dreams, they break down, they find God or even go on an adventure. Yet, what most presume as normal doesn't apply to her. She wasn't normal, not even a little bit.

I've replayed the moment she told me the news. I remembered crying, not because I was sad, but because I was so angry. I was real deal pissed off. I was mad that my brother was torn up behind it, mad because that same day she tried to be manipulative, angry because she thought it would erase her past wrongs only to excuse her new ones. Mostly, I was pissed that I finally broke free from her; in fact, I was numb to her as a whole, and I couldn't share her pain in the manner most in my position would have. She used to say on several occasions that I would need her before she would ever need me. Man, oh man, God has a way to humble a person. She now needed me, in more ways than one. But I couldn't be there for her, not how I should've been. She stripped away my normal emotions, and I was disappointed about it.

For years, I yearned for her love and approval. Deep down, I always knew she didn't like me. My mom was disappointed in who I had become. And although I knew it, I just needed to hear her say it. If I heard it, then it was true. Not sure if I truly understood what that confirmation would do for me. I just knew that it would be my confirmation.

I finally got what I was hoping to receive. She finally came out and said it. But she didn't tell me to my face. She decided to wait until I was miles away, to tell my husband that she would always love me but didn't like the person I'd become. And she didn't stop there. She even told my husband that I wasn't good with our kids. Who does that? No seriously, who in their right mind would say something so foul.

That was the straw that broke the camel's back. I decided to fancy myself and ask her face to face, to make sure my husband didn't misconstrue her words. Sure enough, she boastfully looked me in my eyes and repeated the very words he relayed to me. And at that moment, she was just like anyone else that I erased and replaced. Only she wasn't just anyone; she was my mother. That hit differently.

So, I adjusted my mentality and accepted her for who she is. She's my mother. A narcissist. She's incapable of change. And unable to express pure love. Still, despite how hard it was to accept, those revelations showed me the path to the door that I needed to shut. And like my girl NeNe Leakes said, "THE DOOR IS CLOSED."

So, I appreciate her telling me she loves me. Unfortunately, I don't yearn to hear those words anymore. I appreciate her telling me she is proud of me. Unfortunately, I no longer need her recognition to validate my worth. I understand her desire to put the past behind her and focus on starting fresh. Unfortunately, starting fresh requires a conscious effort to change, and she has not changed. So, while I appreciate her efforts, it's a little too late.

Misplaced Protection

Slavery was abolished over 400 years ago, yet somehow our minds are forever enslaved. I can only speak to the strides my generation has made to rid themselves of the Jim Crow stranglehold, but we are a long way from freedom. The main issue is that from generation to generation, the ideologies trickle-down, which taints the space to evolve. Consider my family the epitome of systematic mental oppression. If I had a dollar for every time, I heard the phrase, "What happens in this house, stays in this house," I would be a millionaire. It is so ass-backward and promotes a level of secrecy that causes real harm. Honestly, I wish that statement died with slavery.

When I entered adulthood, I realized that families love a good scandal. Even more so, they would rather play make-believe, to maintain a good public perception. In layman's terms, they would do anything to save face. I'm no innocent party, due to being taught this behavior for so long, I did it quite often. But what did that teach me? It was sending the message that public image mattered more than actually facing an issue. So, if I was taught this, this meant it was generational toxicity spread miles wide across my family. How could I expect better from them when it was already deeply embedded? I don't know what better looked like. Just know I expected better.

If I have to place blame, it'll be with my grandparents. Because if I'm honest, they created a monster. Monsters create monsters, PERIOD! Outwardly, they didn't appear scary. My grandparents were wolves dressed in sheep's clothing. Not easily detected at first, but like anything in disguise, their true colors were revealed.

They taught my mom everything she knew. But it came back to bite them in the ass. The whole time they penetrated her mind with what they considered normal, they had no earthly inkling that she was a narcissist. So, what happens when you combine bull shit morals with a person who manipulates and devours anyone of which they are acquainted? You are left with pure evil. I'm talking, Seed of Chucky, type of evil.

My grandparents were no exception to her wrath. They enabled her and led her to believe that she was righteous. The addition of dressing to a salad makes it taste better, but it doesn't erase that at its core, it's still just salad. They were aware that she did cruel things but continuously justified her actions because they felt that underneath it all, her intentions were good, and that is ridiculous. They gave her a Band-Aid mindset. She may get a deep cut, but instead of getting stitches, just throw a Band-Aid on it, and give it time to heal on its own. And that shaped her.

My grandparents held secrets, some that my mother witnessed, and others that she didn't. They have that 'put family first' mindset, but I never felt like they put me first. Both accepted outsiders if they conformed to their norms, and for those who didn't, they would send their daughter to get them in line. So, where did that leave the granddaughter that never fit in? Harms' way was an understatement. It was no surprise that my mom tried to rewrite my life. Sometimes it was verbal; other times, it was physical and often both simultaneously. No matter the method, it was dangerous and unwanted. I tried to escape her wrath by asking my grandparents to take me into their home. But they never showed up.

Still, each week they would come by as if I'd never asked to be saved. Each encounter they would talk about her messed up ways as a way to acknowledge that they somewhat felt my pain. Yet, my agony didn't move their hearts to rescue me. I remained in her custody, feeling all alone, still in harm's way. I assumed they left me there out of fear, or at least that's the only explanation that my mind was willing to accept.

When my brother would get in trouble for doing something stupid, he would call them, and like clockwork, they'd come running to his rescue. Time after time, it never failed, he would call, and they would come. It was done so effortlessly. Yet, I'd repeatedly ask them to save me, and like ghosts, they would make themselves invisible to my cries for help. I guess they thought since they were in proximity, that somehow that kept me safe. Well, let me set the record straight for old time's sake. It wasn't enough.

Eventually, I moved away—the relationship I once had with my grandparents began to fade. I started to see the effects of it all, and it was making me sick. Then one day I mustered up the courage to ask my grandmother why she and my grandfather never came, why hadn't they saved me? Her excuse still gives me pause. She said, "She is my daughter, what was I supposed to do." I hung up the phone and yelled, "The fuck you mean, what were you supposed to do…I don't know granny, maybe pick me up before I fucking died!"

But then I realized, my grandparents and mom were the same. They were monsters too, so why would they have helped me. They had lived through their abuse and scandal. They forgave it, and their children witnessed it. It was all an illustration of systematic warfare, and I was just collateral damage.

Much like collateral damage, aftershock causes latent destruction that people experience following a massive earthquake. Too often, we hear stories of the aftershock causing residual damage, that despite its decreased strength, still wreaks havoc on all it touches, which brings me to my dad. My dad was my "truth" teller. He was there every day in that dysfunctional home, as my only ally. Every day he complained, and I felt vindicated in my disgust of my mom's craziness. He allowed me to vent, so I always felt like I had at least one person in my corner. He, too, had massive blowouts with my mom, some worse than others. All were ugly enough to leave, yet he never left, meaning I never left. He is still in the situation to this day.

Part of me believes he told me about his true identity because he wanted me to know. But the other part of me knows it was for his selfish reasons. I mean let's keep it a buck, I was eleven. There is no way in his right mind he thought it was appropriate to not only tell me that he was my dad but also tell me a plethora of adult details about my mom that I shouldn't have heard. As I reflected, it became clear; he wanted to hurt my mom because he felt played. Game recognizes game, and she played the game how it goes. But just like most men, he let his ego take over, and he didn't care who it hurt in the process.

But at some point, his selfish scheme became water under the bridge. But it opened the floodgates. My dad worked so much that he didn't have to deal with her gunfire full time. My brother graduated at some point, and it was just me. I was the punching bag for all her emotions, and she always landed her punches. In her absence, when he and I were alone, he would always tell me how crazy she was and how she had to be stopped. This would be a much better story if he had a master plan, and we made our escape. While that would have been awesome, it was certainly not my reality. He didn't stop her. He never honestly tried. When up against my mom, my dad is the cliché tough guy in the heat of the moment - all bark but no bite. It became a never-ending cycle that would stand to serve me no justice and was the opposite of what I needed. I needed his protection. I needed him to be my shield. I needed him to save me. But he never did.

So many times, my mom would do something absurd, and my dad would tell me if he were there, it wouldn't have gone down like that. He sometimes came home and argued with her to show that he had my back, but he never left her, nor did he have any intent to stage our exit. What I came to realize is that he was making excuses for his inability to protect me adequately.

It became clear when I got older. He was damaged, and like my grandparents, he lived for turmoil and dysfunction. I mean, he does have seven kids and five baby mamas, so I should've known. He didn't protect me because he was protecting his heart. He didn't save me because he had to use me to slow her down. He had a plan, and I was a key factor in its execution. Only, it didn't slow her down. It made the flame bigger. It intensified her power. He was a goon, but she was a goblin. He never stood a chance and never will.

I used to see my dad as my best friend because he let me curse, he let me vent, and I thought he was the only person who accepted me for me. But he wasn't my best friend, he was my dad, and he used me. And if we are going to call a spade a spade, then let's call it as we see it. My dad was a COWARD, and he should've done better.

The Elephant in the Room

Since I was a small child, I felt like an outsider. As if I was the puzzle piece that didn't seem to fit. I always knew that my family was different. But I had no other family to compare them to and no one to question or challenge the things they considered normal. You see, my family has a lot of norms. Not the typical ancestral traditions and myths, we read about or watched in movies. They have a view on how life works and how people should operate. Any person whose actions were outside their scope of norms was considered a person that did not value themselves or lacked home training.

To make the picture clearer, I'll share a few examples. My family would say the weather was all clear until you were ready to travel. If you didn't tell your parents where you were at all times, or you lied, and you were found dead, your parents wouldn't believe the police because you didn't say that you were there.

We have all heard the sayings "I know what they did was messed up, but that's your family" or "you only get one mother, so make it right." I cannot stand those statements. But the worst of them all is "Blood is thicker than water." If I could make one thing in life disappear, it would be that exact statement. Hell, throw the whole sentence away. I mean duhhhh, we know blood is thicker than water, but what does that even mean? More importantly, why does that justify accepting "fuckery" from fucked up family? If you ask the twenty-eight-year-old me, she would've had an excuse, but not today.

There is no truth when correlating family with blood. One thing I know for sure is that we can't choose the family we are born into. However, what we can choose is the family that matters most. And that husband of mine matters most to me.

The most important part of gaining a life partner is that you get the right to CHOOSE. You have control over your emotions, and you have the power to give up access. When choosing your spouse, you intentionally allow that person to invade your mental space with the closest access to your emotional well-being. That's MAJOR!

Often, I wondered how my husband handled always being the most hated guy in the room. He had this way about him that screamed, "TRY ME." What's truly funny is that no one ever did. Now I mentioned before how a weak mind is a narcissist playground, making a strong mind their biggest nightmare. I like to think of him as my sweet dream and my mother's beautiful nightmare. He caught her off guard with his willpower and unwillingness to be altered. He frightened her in a way that others couldn't. My husband had control, and it made my mom lose control. But the scariest thing he did to her was shifting the atmosphere around her daughter, a shift that allowed her daughter to see herself in a better light, a transformation that gave room for her daughter to find her authentic voice. And finally, a shift that helped break the shackles of her daughter's soul. I'm sure she will hate him forever for it. But she will be aight!!!

I bet when my husband met me, he didn't envision having to be my emotional bodyguard. I know we all think that our mate should be ready to safeguard our emotions at all costs. But that doesn't mean they should be expected to drown in them. But my husband dove in headfirst. He was my life vest when I couldn't stay afloat. He was my oxygen when I felt like I couldn't breathe. I exhausted him. I drained him beyond any imaginable capacity, and even at that moment, he found more strength to allow me to get to my point of growth. And I am thankful he stood by me.

I remember our first few dates. He noticed my anger and made me identify it. He saw my lack of originality and made me figure out my thoughts. He noticed that I was beautiful inside and out, so he made sure I recognized it too. I don't think I ever truly realized how much he opened my eyes, but now they are as wide as the Grand Canyon.

We used to have the same argument over and over. I would always get mad when he would tell me he didn't need me. I mean, how could he say that?! Hell, I needed him. It took me a while, but now I understand. I don't need him. I just wanted to need him.

During the time that I needed him, I had time to grow. He always stood in front of me, taking every blow so that I didn't have to suffer. He is not perfect, and we have gone through some things. But he is the definition of a rider. "Alexa, tell me the perfect example of a ride or die," I swear his name will be her answer.

The one principle that he lives by truly irks my nerves, but it's necessary. He always says go with your move and live with the consequences. It only irritates me when his move is to ignore me, but at least he is consistent. I see why most of my family dislikes him. It's his mind. It's his unwavering sense of self. It's his ability never to fake his feelings. My husband is built differently, and my family can't stand it.

My family knew my husband had my back. Not the normal chime in on a discussion to come to my defense, type of back up. I'm talking about parking his car in the living room of anyone who mistreats me, kind of back up. The depth of how hard he comes behind me is unmatched. They admired how much he loved me and how much he uplifted me. At the same time, they found it disrespectful. How dare he only love me and not care to be around them!! He is so solid that they would make up things to rally around just to justify the hate they had for him. The simple fact that they tried everything to stop our wedding. I mean, literally tried to tank it as I started to walk down the aisle. But one thing I'll never forget about our wedding day was while they were trying to ruin it, I entered that aisle, and as I looked up, there he was smiling so big. Crazy thing is he was so mad at me that day, yet he didn't hesitate to say I do. I guess he knew that better days were coming, even if I was too blind to see it.

I've honestly never met anyone more wise or grounded. He loved me when I didn't love myself. He fought my battles when I had no fight left. But mostly, he accepted me as an outsider, showed me that I wasn't crazy for thinking my family was abnormal, and allowed me to grow into the woman I am today. He made sure my family knew that even in my darkest hour, I would never be alone. He checks all the boxes, and I'll love him forever!

Chapter 2

Let's Not Confuse the Facts

"I am not afraid of my truth anymore and I will not omit pieces of me to make you comfortable."

Mood

Triggered (Remix) - Jhene Aiko, 21 Savage & Summer Walker
Fly Before You Fall - Cynthia Erivo
When I Was Down - OMB Peezy
Love Yourself - Justin Bieber

You never lose a friend. I read that once on an Instagram post, and I internalized it. But what does it mean? In my mind, it meant that if someone were your true friend, they would never stop being your friend. But what is a "true friend"? Frankly, I don't think I know the answer. I don't know the answer because friendship stems from relationships, and I hadn't had any good examples. Without a good example of a good relationship, recognizing a bad relationship is surely harder to pinpoint.

Now listen, I for one think I am awesome; but in reality I am an acquired taste. Many people came and went out of my life. Some left due to distance, others due to differences in our outlook on life, and a couple left because it turns out I just wasn't their cup of tea. I guess that's the Libra in me replaying all failed friendships during my lifetime, weighing out my faults versus the other person's faults. If I caused the downfall, then I could accept my wrongs, but if the other person was the problem, then I needed a definite conclusion to feel justified. A winner had to be declared. Sadly, most times, even when the list showed that I hadn't been the problem, subconsciously, I would think I was wrong. In some cases, that feeling of guilt would cause me to reach out to the very person that I should've left in my past.

So why did I feel guilty? Why did I always feel the need to revive an extinguished flame? Why did I feel the need always to be the bigger person?

We all have crossed paths with a moment in life, where we ask ourselves, why does this keep happening to me? More often than none, we can pinpoint the exact moment. Other times we are too blind to see what's right before our eyes, and in rare cases, we have not dug deep enough to reveal the authentic answer. Well, let's just say I embodied all three of those reasons, but mostly I had never dug deep enough to get to the root of it all. Sometimes we don't search for the truth because we have fixed ourselves to believe that it's just the way life goes. Funny thing about life is that righteousness always presents itself, mostly when you aren't looking for it.

Yep, you guessed it.

The answer to my questions found me. One sentence unveiled years and years of truths. Let me say that again. One sentence revealed several years of facts about my failed friendships. I would've wished that this came to me sooner, but then we wouldn't be here at this moment discussing this would we.

Alright, so let me run it down to you.

Typically, your first friend, if you are lucky enough, is your older sibling. They teach the ins and outs of this thing we call life. Even if it's completely fucked up and sends you down the path of immense destruction, they still take on the role of your "cool" tour guide. Some good examples are from my childhood favorites, Fresh Prince, Family Matters, and Moesha. Each show you would see the siblings' fuss and fight, but overall, they shared bonds that were unbreakable, genuine, and mutually beneficial.

So, of course, that was my expectation. If the kids on tv had that, then I should have that too, right? I guess I started compensating for things I lacked early without realizing it. Clearly, my expectations were low. I mean, they had to be for me to not see my brother for what he was.

All this time I thought we were thick as thieves. He called every morning around six a.m. I'd have to sneak in the other room to answer, so I didn't wake the kids. He would talk his shit, and I'd talk him down from doing something irrational. We were consistent, so I assumed we were solid. I mean hell, he's my brother. Well, you know what they say about people who make assumptions.

I guess I never sat back to realize the dynamic of those early morning conversations. He literally would call and vent for a good thirty minutes. He never asked how I was doing, if I had any ongoing life issues, how my kids were doing, and damn sure didn't ask if I needed anything. In fact, he never invited me to his home, outside of holiday shindigs.

But then one day, I had lunch with his wife and our mom. My mom asked her why they never invited my husband and me to their couple nights and trips. She replied, "Your brother said ya'll aren't even close like that." I looked at mom and then back at her in absolute shock. In my head, I'm screaming, "I know you fucking lying." It was a total slap in the face. Stunned is the word to describe my reaction, and even that word doesn't truly encompass the level of betrayal I felt.

It was at that moment that I began to take a closer look at the relationship we shared. Any person on the outside could call it for what it was without a second guess. It was always evident. My vision was off. I yearned for the brother-sister relationship that I saw my friends have with their siblings. I wanted for that feeling so much to the point that any interaction we had that remotely resembled it, I would let that moment outweigh the reality. The truth is my brother never showed me love. He never provided protection.

He never offered guidance. And above all, he was CONSISTENT at being INCONSISTENT.

In any scenario where there is a lack of consistency, you see a rise in contentment. You typically hear of a situation where there is an absent parent, particularly a father figure. The father promises the child he will come to visit on a particular day, then on the day of the promise he flakes. The father presents some lame excuse for the repetitive neglect and the child, while outwardly seems accepting, internally has mentally trained themself to see this behavior as normal. This becomes a cycle. This shapes future encounters and creates acceptance of what we will henceforth call the "bullshitter.

So, there it is, we have established that my brother is a bullshitter.

But this didn't all start as we became adults. This started as early as I can remember. During our childhood days, he was my first bully. I guess because he was a follower, he needed to know what it was like to be a leader. I was young and just happy to be around, so I followed him. We always did what he wanted when he wanted. He would dismiss me when his friends came around but act like we were best friends, while still getting his way when only the two of us were around.

I mean, we did everything that benefited him. My brother desperately needed to feel dominant, so I learned to be submissive. Servient is the best word to describe it. But he allowed me to be around. So submissive is the key. Got it!

Not only had I become the servant in his life, but I also had my first taste of what it's like to feel inferior. I remember, like it was yesterday, my brother said to me, "I look better than you because I am light skin, and you are dark skin." We had to have at least been like 12 and 14 years old. But it didn't stop there. Somehow, he knew that if he always showed me that I was beneath him, I would always find a way to make sure that I stayed in his good grace. I would always feel guilty. Constantly feel the need to make it right even when he was wrong. It also didn't help that our grandparents spoiled him so rotten that he felt invincible. When a person knows that no matter what they do, there is always that certain someone in their corner that will never let them fall, they tend to think they are immortal. Of course, I know he isn't immortal. What I do know is he's a user, selfish, and superficial.

So, guess what type of friends Yladrea accepted in her life?

For the longest, I didn't know why I always made myself small so that others could feel big. Why I let others pick and choose when I was worth their time. Why I allowed these sorts of people around me, but more importantly, why I did whatever it took to make sure they stuck around.

I know now. Thanks to my brother. Actually, thanks to his wife, who shared his vision of whatever the fuck we have.

Despite our differences, I admire his drive and ambition. He's still pretty fly and funny as hell. We don't talk as much, I'm sure he doesn't notice. But we talk whenever he calls or text. Go figure. Overall, nothing about my brother has changed. He's still a user, selfish, and superficial.

But one thing has changed. That change is me. I now know how to describe what we have. I now know why many of my friendships failed. I know how to determine what a friend to me looks like. Finally, I now see where the trend began. Even though he was a follower, he's always been pretty trendy, which makes it easy for him to be a trendsetter naturally.

Thank goodness all trends find their end as a new one begins.

Betrayed by My Past

There were two friends in my life that I cut off cold turkey. I didn't bat an eye at the moment. In fact, in both instances, I didn't revisit the thought for two years. Both were childhood friends. Both were like sisters, and both have never seen me the same 'til this day. But only one, I genuinely feel I have wronged. That's on me, and I have to live with that.

To truly heal, I had to be honest with myself about my wrongs. Despite the outside forces that shaped my way of moving through life, I have to take responsibility. I take responsibility because it isn't someone else's fault that I didn't know how to recognize what a good friendship looked like. It wasn't her fault that I didn't know who I was as a woman. It wasn't her fault that I didn't know how to express myself enough to work through things. And it damn sure wasn't her fault that I was so damaged that in so many ways, I was jealous of her.

So, if you are reading this Peanut, just hear me out.

Many of you will never be born into this world with a friend picked for you. See, our parents were friends since they were in kindergarten, so we didn't have much of a say in the matter. Honestly, I can't complain. She was super dope. She saw me for me. Like really understood me. She was the sister I never had. Well, that's how it felt back then, even though I have three amazing sisters.

Nonetheless, back then, I didn't know them the way I knew her. I remember my sisters were so pissed when I made a post about how she was more of a sister to me than my blood sisters. Whew chileeeee, they were not having it. And rightfully so, it was a tacky post.

She stayed at my house for months at a time. Not because she didn't have a loving family. But because we wanted to do hoodrat shit with our hoodrat friends. And it just so happened that our "hoodrat" friends stayed closer to me. Just so ya'll know, we grew up in the suburbs, ain't much hoodrat activity happening in those streets, but ya'll not about to play us, it was hoodrat shit, and I said what I said.

Anyway, I've had time to deeply reflect on the history of our entire friendship. I've concluded that my reason for cutting her off for two years may have some validity. Be that as it may, when I completed this deep dive into how it all went wrong, there was an overwhelming answer. I was a shitty friend. PERIOD.

She of all people witnessed my mom in her finest hours. She saw how she treated me, and she was a rider. She even endured some of my mom's shit so that I didn't have to face it alone. I would've taken my ass home because my mom was doing the most. But not Peanut. She was right there.

My brother didn't switch up his behavior towards her, either. He was the same selfish person to her that he was to me because he too treated her like his little sister. Yet, there she was, fighting him with me, dealing with his nonsense and assisting me in my many midnight attacks on him when he fell asleep.

Still, I didn't recognize the depth of our friendship. I didn't stop to see how much she was in my corner. As a matter of fact, I repaid her by either dating all of her exes or trying to steal her current boyfriends. I tried to upstage her presence at school, even though she was always more popular. I had learned to lie so much that I lied to her when all she wanted was the truth. Then when the truth came out during our adulthood, I shitted on her feelings. I dismissed her hurt, and I told her to grow up.

But that's what my relationships with my family members taught me. It taught me that you could lie, do horrible things, and in the end, people should just get over it. But she didn't get over it, and she shouldn't be expected to.

I treated her the way my brother treated me. I wanted to feel dominant. I wanted to feel superior. I wanted to be big and finally not feel small. For years I blamed her for why we aren't as close. Like I real deal felt like it was her loss. But it wasn't her loss; it was mine. Quite frankly, I didn't deserve her friendship.

I've learned that hurt people hurt people. Whether it is intentional or unintentional, when people are hurt, they can't help but rain on everyone's parade. It's in the moment that they are past that hurt that they look back and see the destruction they caused. So here I am a few steps beyond my pain, and I'd like to believe that I hurt her because I was hurting. I caused her pain because I was in pain. All the same, regardless of my reason, it was unacceptable.

And for whatever it's worth, I'm genuinely sorry.

Keep That Same Energy

When people show you who they are, believe them. Crazy thing is, I've always shown who I was, but one person, in particular, chose not to believe me.

Anyone who truly knows me will tell you that I am not judgmental. They will also tell you that I am brutally honest. I know, I know people say that all the time, but I am serious, my honesty is award-winning. I am also very transparent. I used to think that made me a prize or a person that anyone would want to be friends with. WRONG!

All those traits can be massive turn-offs to some people. Mostly, I've found that it makes me the worst kind of person for someone innately judgmental. She was judgmental, like extremely. She admitted it and never shied away from the fact. When she first met me, I told her something that she felt was too transparent for a first-time encounter, and she stayed her distance. I guess, over time, she felt the need to improve in the area of judgment because others made her feel like it was a flaw. So, she chose to give friendship with me a chance.

But sis should've gone with her gut.

You see, she didn't know the years of baggage I had to unpack. Her view on life stemmed from the examples set before her by her parents, life experiences, instilled morals, and strong religious beliefs. Which by the way, there is nothing wrong with. I, myself, viewed life through the examples set before me too. The big difference is that the majority of mine were undeniably crappy.

For so long, I was trained to be silent, trained to keep secrets. Trained to follow familial norms, in which I was taught not to accept those who thought differently. But the worst part of it all is I was trained to save face. So, I guess it was my instinct to be the total opposite when I grew older and left the nest. I truly felt like the only thing I could control was my narrative. So, I made a promise to myself to always be an open book. I was intentional about it, and I won't apologize for it.

But it isn't all good. That honesty and transparency allowed many to take advantage of me. It also caused me to cut off my sense of discernment and timing of when to say or not say things. It sometimes was so bad that I would say things without even recognizing it. Some of those things were hurtful, and some things needed to be heard. In the end, I never hid these characteristics. I also don't feel the need to hold a sign that reads: Enter at your own risk!

So, here's the deal. I feel like she was selfish, and lowkey used me until she didn't need me anymore. I'm not even mad, and here is why:

Through our time as friends, I learned so much about myself that I wouldn't have otherwise learned if I'd never lived through it. It also was the first friendship that showed me that I had an actual purpose and the ability to be used for that purpose. It stirred up familiar feelings from my relationship with my brother that opened my eyes. Mostly, it showed me that some friendships are meant to last for a season, and that's necessary.

Let me get more specific. I felt that she was selfish because she needed a moral compass of some sort. She needed to prove to herself that she was not as judgmental by enduring friendship with me. My transparency and honesty about myself caused her to be conflicted so many times. I was unfiltered, raw, and uncut 24/7. That became a huge problem down the line. At the same time, that openness gave her room to be her true self around me. She can deny it if she wants, but she was completely free to be the rawest version of herself, free of guilt and judgment when she was around me. I know that she appreciated that.

However, she was embarrassed by me. She always felt the need to warn her other friends or family about me before I came around. She would coach me on the tone of the audience before I entered the premises and give me guidelines to stay within. So,

I was good enough when it was just her and me, but a nuisance when in mixed company. I couldn't put my finger on how that made me feel until now. It reminded me of how my family used to coach me on how to act before I went around their friends. It told me of how my mom would talk shit about me to her friends just so that if I did something wrong, she would have already pre-excused my behavior. It reminded me of the captivity I experienced under my childhood roof. It was absurd and hurtful.

She'll probably want to know why I felt used. Well, as I stated earlier, I showed her who I was from the jump. I cheered her on like I was her biggest fan. I shared some of the lowest and most vulnerable moments of my life. Granted her access to things extremely personal to me. Yet, in the end, she shitted on me.

She finally reached the level of success she dreamed about, and shortly after I didn't fit into that picture. I was honest about how her success caused me to feel jealous because I hadn't even scratched the surface of my dreams. But she didn't reassure me. She didn't help me find my way. I mean, she extended help, but it was just enough to give her room to say she tried. But it wasn't genuine. Her help began to come with similar comments like, "I don't want to hear anything when it doesn't work out because I am telling you my way worked." It was back-handed help, and I wish she would've kept it.

At last, she started to reveal her true feelings that she held in for what seemed like years. She would start petty arguments that allowed her to explode on me. She would use these times to justify or warrant the harsh comments she'd say to me. She would try to say comments like, "I should've told you sooner," so that she didn't feel bad about saying it in the present moment. But in reality, it was tasteless and not cool at all. But she wanted me to receive it and adapt. Sad thing is that, as an emotional libra, I would internalize it and try to adjust to appease her feelings even when she was dead ass wrong. I still can't believe I allowed that.

In between times of silence and arguments, she would reach out to me in the same manner that I watched her do to people that she no longer truly liked. In one instance, she knew the answer, but she texts me to feel the gratification of my failure and give herself the right to say, "I told you so." It was disgusting, and I should've recognized the shift in respect at that moment. But I was trying to convince myself that it wasn't what I presumed it to be. Another fucked up trait I learned from my family, giving people the benefit of the doubt where it isn't warranted.

Now let's talk about the grand finale of that friendship. I get to our sit down thinking she was coming to apologize for what I considered hater behavior. But babyyyyyyyy she had another agenda. My girl sat at that table, looked me dead in my eyes and said, "I think that I am just now realizing that I never really liked you as a person," followed by more unsettled feelings on topics that were petty, and with an ending ask of "but I hope that we can work through this."

Say what now? Come again? Girl, you triedddddddddd it!

At the moment, I was so confused and hurt. I was like how dare she! I felt used and abused all at the same time. I knew there was no point of return. I walked away from that restaurant and never looked back.

I want all of you to look long and hard at the statement that my girl said to me at that table. Sounds familiar doesn't it? Honestly, I think that this moment hardened me, and when my mother said similar words, it sealed the deal. Everyone doesn't deserve access to your value because once it no longer serves them, they will get rid of you quicker than an eraser.

So, I'm thankful for that moment. I needed it for my growth. I needed it to open my mind. I needed it as a reference to what I don't need nor want. So, while I will always cherish the friendship we had, I am so glad it's over.

II. Failing Forward

Chapter 3

Delayed Not Denied

"When you doubt your power, you give power to your doubt."
- Honore De Balzac

Mood

On My Mind - Jorja Smith & Preditah
All Falls Down - Kanye West
I Love Me - Demi Lovato
I'll Show You - Justin Bieber

So, there I stood on the side of the commencement stage, waiting for my moment. They called my name, and across the stage, I walked. I should've run just in case they tried to take the degree back. When people say to me, "Wow, that's awesome that you graduated from law school," I always respond, sometimes out loud and other times in my head, BARELLLLLLLLYYYY! Truth is, I wasn't an A student, hell not even a B student. But guess what, I got that J to the damn D. And no one can take that from me.

When I entered law school, I was twenty-one years old. No one in my family had ever gone, so I didn't know what to expect. I was so green. I remember the first day of orientation. I pulled up to the door and noticed everyone dressed in a suit. I had on jeans and a t-shirt. Clearly, I missed the memo. I hurried back to my apartment and changed into the most professional outfit I could find. I hadn't bought not one suit. Honestly, it never crossed my mind.

So, let's tap into this legal journey.

It all went by so fast. The first year went by, and I noticed that I unquestionably hated law school. I recall thinking, if this is any representation of what an attorney does in real life, I don't want it. Return to sender, you hear me. For those who don't know, not all who start with you will finish with you. To that end, the first year is what I call the chopping block. But by some miracle, I made the cut. So I decided to give it another shot to impress me. You heard me right. I wanted to be impressed. I wanted to see some first season of Suits type of shit! Not one shiny bell or whistle was shown to me, so they had some work to do.

Year two rolls around, and I guess I adjusted and began drinking the Kool-Aid. I started to get more competitive in my grades and tried to get more involved. I figured the only way to wholeheartedly take in the experience, was to throw myself into the thick of it. My law school was filled with very successful attorneys who had thriving careers. They were known for employing some of the toughest professors in the state. And for producing some of the best courtroom attorneys. But thassssssssit! Nothing more, nothing less.

The motto of the law center was "Seriousness of Purpose." Now, if you ask any of the professors at the school, what that means, I can bet you ten million dollars that all will say something different. I guarantee it. Why though? Because the shit doesn't make a lick of sense. However, during my time at the school, they used it as a measure of excellence. Let them tell it. It was the gold standard that we all should strive to achieve.

We were pit against each other to strive to get the highest rank or G.P.A. in the class. They never shied away from letting us know that those at the top get the good jobs, the most interviews, and gain the most access. Those at the top were able to get more scholarships and more internship opportunities. So, if you weren't in the top ten percent, you basically weren't shit. Simple. That dynamic was problematic and unrealistic. Not only did my school cater to the top percent, but it also shared its dissatisfaction with those who were in the lower half. Continuously telling us, we needed to try harder, apply ourselves more, and learn from our peers at the top. We were all crabs in a bucket, clawing our way towards the top, and they were fueled by it.

Check this out. Those at the bottom were kept in the dark about several internships. Additionally, we were kept from many introductions to successful alums and invitations to some of the professors, outside of school-sanctioned events. We were on the outside looking in. We were able to collect the tickets but never allowed to enjoy the show. Once again, I was an outsider, and the shit was getting old.

But guess what we were invited to? We were invited to the tuition office and the bookstore. We were invited to buy school paraphernalia and parking passes. We were asked to pay for tickets to the barrister's ball and anything else where money was involved. Even though we weren't worth the investment, they would let us stick around so that the doors wouldn't close.

So here I sit with over 200,000 dollars in student loan debt, and yes, their doors are still open.

Oh Okay! Cool. I' ma let them make it. Because despite the law centers flaws, it still awarded me my degree. And despite what my rank says to them, I know I worked my ass off for it.

Nevertheless, I made it through year three and went on to graduate. I was twenty-four years old on the day I graduated. It was one of the highest moments of my life. Look at me, a twenty-four-year-old black woman with a Juris Doctor, ready to take on the world. That moment only lasted for about a week. I started to realize that I had been moving at full speed through school and had never even had a real adult job. I had no idea of the road ahead or what was next.

All I knew was that the law center geared our minds with the following steps: Graduate law school, prepare for the bar, take the bar, pass the bar, become an attorney, then go forth and be great. The end. That's the goal. That's what it means to have a "seriousness of purpose."

Along the path, I went. Scratching off tasks as they were completed.

Graduate, check. Prepare for the bar, check. Take the bar, check. Retake the bar, check. And again, check.

Not pass the bar, check. Don't become an attorney, check. I guess I don't go forth and be great, CHECK!

I took the bar three times before; I got my mind right and realized I never cared to take it in the first place. But that was the standard, and I needed to meet it. I had a burning desire to prove the law center and naysayers wrong. I was smart, I deserve my degree, and I was going to succeed. But that's just it, I was all those things, but I wanted validation.

I recognized this feeling. The feeling of needing to prove my value, my worth. The sense of self-doubt and fear of never being good enough. I didn't come to law school to add to my self-doubt, to my inability to see my worth and to the constant feeling of never being good enough. But that's what my school had to offer. That was their tactic to breed winners and weed out losers. It was wack. And I hope for those that came behind me that they changed their ways.

In the spirit of setting standards, I would like for them to know they failed many of us, but I am here to talk about how they failed me.

For starters, they were lazy. It doesn't take much effort to provide their students with career alternatives that stem from our degree. I sucked at moot court. I wasn't quick on my feet, and I didn't want to deliver a sermon. It just wasn't for me. I thought I wanted to be a sports agent, but they only supplied us with one internship in that arena, coupled with actual sports agents whom made sure we knew it was a man's world. I mean damn what's a girl to do just to get some options.

I wanted to learn how to write laws, not defend them. I wanted to know how to keep people compliant or how to make sure all actions in the workplace followed the rules and were legally sound. But they didn't give me those alternatives. It was either become an attorney or get left behind.

To further that divide, there is an entire alumni group on Facebook that we gain access to once we graduate. But let's be honest the group is really for those who pass the bar. No one is checking for us who don't.

Which leads me to my next point - they left me for dead and never cared to check for a pulse.

How Sway, you ask?

A Juris Doctor degree is a blessing and a curse. It's a blessing because it displays that you know an area that is difficult to learn. It's a curse because if you don't pass the bar exam, you are either overqualified or underqualified. It's never in between in case you were wondering. But they knew that. They knew that jobs are hard to come by without that bar roll number. They also knew that they hadn't prepared us to pass any and every bar exam. Indeed, they were inadequate but chose to make me think it was the other way around. All I'm saying is, if they didn't believe I was a good investment, then they should've let me take my exit. But they strung me along. Then when I didn't reach the level of expectation set for me, they turned their back and walked away. Well, not completely away. They still send emails to me asking for me to give my coins, even though they never checked to see if I had any. But I digress.

Finally, I want to retouch on the fact that they purposely created self-doubt and provided us with the standard of worth. What does that do for them? Is that the only way to teach us the law?

For so long, I equated success with passing the bar exam. When I failed, I would go into this state of depression. I would feel like my life was pointless and that I had no worth. I mean, we studied for about three months for a three-day exam, then wait three months for the results. Only to find out publicly that you didn't pass. You just weren't good enough. Then imagine not passing it more than once. You experience that feeling over and over.

I can't help but wonder if I had been presented with alternatives, would I have felt so low. Would I have found another way to utilize my skills, and would I have noticed that success doesn't end and begin with a bar roll number? I'm sure that I wouldn't have because once I broke that concept in my brain, I've never felt better.

Sometimes we need negativity to spark a fire in our soul. I needed it to entice my mental strength. I needed it to force me to figure out what I wanted in life. And I needed it to stand up and fight, to show how resilient I can be. And I'm pretty tough if I do say so myself.

Still, they likely will attribute my success to the degree they awarded me. They will probably believe that they were a key factor in my come up. And while they provided me with a great skill set, they damn sure didn't get me here. So, kill that thought, and kill it quick.

Mind Over Matter

It's something about failing the bar exam that tells my ovaries it's time to create a child. I dodged the trend one out of the three L's I took. But the other two, I was blessed with both of my babies. I'm so lucky to be their mother. As much as I don't want to admit it, I didn't always see it that way.

My husband grew up around a large, tight-knit family. He had experience with babysitting and watching kids. His family truly believed in the need for a village to raise a child. They didn't care about material things or money. They just knew that everyone needed to eat, and everyone needed a place to sleep. It was never a task to watch each other's kids, nor was it an expectation. It was just what they did. Sure, they had all kinds of family drama, and not all parents were present, but still, they all learned how to take care of each other. So, when it came to having kids, my husband wanted a football team.

Similarly, I grew up around a large, tight-knit family. But I don't know what happened to my generation. We just didn't get that babysitting phase. I never changed a diaper until I was about five months pregnant with my first child. I never was interested in anything surrounding a baby. I also didn't think I would have kids, just wasn't in the cards.

I trained my mind not to want kids. I mean, I was pretty screwed up mentally, I had no business having kids. I was scared that I would turn out like my mom, just angry and hurting them both in the process. So, I put the deck away.

We all know the saying, "If you want to make God laugh, tell him your plans." I know God must've thought he was a comedian, because there I was at twenty-five, pregnant with baby number one, a few days after finding out I had just failed the bar exam. I was so terrified and disappointed.

I not only felt worthless but now I was pregnant dealing with morning sickness and pregnancy brain. I couldn't sit for the next bar exam, and I was behind schedule.

Granted, I was one of the lucky graduates who found a paralegal job right after the bar exam. So, I did have a job, but it wasn't the goal. So, let's see, I failed the bar exam, I now have a job which would hinder study time, and I am pregnant with morning sickness. Sounds like a recipe for disaster, or at least that's how I saw it at that time.

In my husband's eyes, they were a big blessing. Yet to me, as painful as this is to write, my oldest son was a major setback.

To make matters worse, I was laid off from my job. Not even a month later, he was born.

It took a couple of days for it to hit me that he was my child, I was his mother, and he was the priority. Just when I was coming to grips with reality, I experienced late preeclampsia, causing me to have a seizure, with the discovery of an aneurysm. Nothing scared me more than the idea that he would grow up without me. But I made it through.

Still, when I returned home, I was timid and had no clue how to take care of my baby. His dad took the lead as he always did and helped me learn how to handle him. I got better with time.

But as he grew, so did my self-doubt. I was jobless and broke. I retook the bar exam and failed. But this time, it wasn't just a failure for me. I had failed him. I was so stuck in that failure that I became angry. I would get mad at him for no reason, and that was not fair. I was turning into the very person I feared I would be. I was becoming a mild version of my mom, and that just wasn't going to work.

I was missing out on how awesome he was. Yes, I was present, but I wasn't living in the moment. My mind was cloudy. I was in a negative space. After all, I didn't know my self-worth or a way to make him proud. I had an obligation to give him the world and show him, love. But I couldn't.

Here's the thing, I had no clue what a mother's love was, I never knew my worth, and everything outside of his dad increased my self-doubt. I was a hot ass mess. My son deserved better, but I didn't know how to be better.

Something had to change, and it needed to change fast.

At some point, I saw a glimmer of light. I put on my big girl panties and woman'd the fuck up. Don't get it twisted I was still an emotional roller coaster, but at least I found some fight.

Hurricane Harvey was a horrible time for most here in Houston. Ya'll forgive me when I say this, but that storm came right on time. That disaster created a job for me. I hadn't worked in over a year. And then boom out of the ashes I came. On the flip side, my job required me and others with a J.D. to help those impacted by Harvey and get them back into their homes. So, we moved to Dallas, and the tides began to turn. The hours were long, and the environment was annoying, but for the first time, I was using my degree, providing for my family, and helping others. Things were looking up.

It's crazy how a change in scenery can change how you view the scene. Being in Dallas created a bubble of bliss for our family. It was so blissful it almost had me thinking I could live there. Dallas is cool or whatever, but that's going to be a no for me. Nonetheless, it was a place where I could get a new perspective. It was a place that wasn't attached to my past trauma. It symbolized new beginnings and fresh starts. The best part of the new city was that I finally had a new mindset. That new mindset let me clear the clouds from my mind and allowed me to focus on what matters. And you, son, mattered the most.

Perfectly Imperfect

Whoever came up with the theory that the first year of marriage is the hardest, you were not lying. But what you didn't mention was that so are all the years after that. Although it shouldn't always be rough, marriage for sure takes work. I like to think of marriage as the Hunger Games, "may the odds be ever in your favor." No bullshit, marriage ain't for the faint-hearted.

So, what makes it so hard?

The answer is simple.

EVERYTHINGGGGGG.

From finances, insecurities, priorities, heightened expectations, down to the simple task of deciding on what restaurant to eat at, it's all bad. The list is endless. The moment you say I do, it's like a switch goes off, and suddenly everything gets serious. Most times, it's the wife, but that's not the case here.

For starters, neither one of us was ready for marriage. What's funny is we both had a personal deadline to get married by the age of twenty-five. His deadline was set so that in the event he met the right person before twenty-five, then he would make it official. Also, if he didn't get married by that time, then he would never get married. Meanwhile, mine was because I had a made-up timeline of what my life would look like. In my head, I would be married at twenty-five, be a successful attorney by twenty-seven, have children at twenty-eight (if I ever decided to have them) and be a millionaire by thirty. Clearly, his reason was more realistic, and mine was just another example of how badly my mental state was distorted.

I'm going to put it out there, people who have timelines aren't always stupid, but as for me, I was foolish. Foolish in a sense that I didn't even know how to love, yet I had the nerve to put a timeline on marriage. I was fascinated by the idea of having it all when I wanted it to happen. But I didn't possess the necessary grit to be somebody's wife.

Characteristics of true grit, according to many sources, means to have courage, strength, and perseverance. I had not a single ounce of any of those characteristics. And I mean not one. I was a perpetrator. I pretended to be down for the home team, but I wasn't even in the dugout. The Home Team is what my husband and I named our family before it even began. I talked a big game, but it was all talk and no action.

To add to that, I didn't possess the proper ingredients to love someone appropriately. Looking at the buildup of my self-doubt from law school, my lack of self-worth from bar failure, and my inability to acknowledge my purpose after losing my job, I was not only sinking. I was drowning. So naturally, I wanted my husband to save me. Marriage is about love, and love conquers all they say. But let's face it, love can't conquer all if you don't know how to love.

To be clear, my husband wasn't ready for marriage, either. But his mentality and grip on his sense of self were solid. He didn't have a real example of what it meant to be a husband. Yet, he was miles ahead of me regarding priorities. Where he lacked took its toll on our marriage, and it furthered my self-doubt, self-worth, and a sense of purpose. I thought that our relationship was strong enough for the transition. Sadly, between his issues and mine, we were not set up to succeed.

My mom always said that a bad financial situation could ruin a marriage. Of course, I didn't want to hear that because of who was delivering the message. I always would be defensive and say that if you love someone, finances won't be an issue. You would've thought I was a marriage counselor the way I would deliver a sermon on the tools to maintain a lasting marriage. I mean, who the hell did I think I was for real. I am laughing so hard as I type this because I vividly remember listing out the steps to success. I was so damn green. It's scary.

Guess whose financial struggles almost ruined their marriage?

Turns out that when financial aid is no longer a big chunk of your finances, you have to get it how you live when you enter the actual adult world. Sad to say, I didn't realize how many bills were associated with adulting, nor did I know that the job market was brutal. What I do know is that adulting is The G.H.E.T.T.O. and I don't like it here.

Here's the thing, finances were only smoke in mirrors to the real issues in my marriage. We experienced infidelity, lack of affection, parenting differences, outside family disruptions, and several other bumps in the road. These issues caused me to pour all of my focus into fighting for my marriage. I mean, I tried everything to hold us together. Emphasis on "I" because I was battling alone.

My husband is stubborn, cold, and definitive to a fault. After losing his mother in the early stages of our relationship that light, I bragged about before started to dim. It dimmed so much until it completely went dark. Over the years, that darkness caused me pain. But as I said before, hurt people hurt people, and he was shattered.

So, there I was trying to ease his pain while he caused me pain. My husband didn't have any fight, and I became so obsessed with trying to be the savior that I neglected all other aspects of my life. From my job search to teaching my son new milestones, it all came second to my need to fix our marriage. I was consumed in the fight without the weapons to win.

Even when I started back working and we began to get on our feet financially, my focus was on the fight. Why was this so hard? Why couldn't we just enjoy our marriage? Suddenly, it hit me. The battle is bigger than me. It is beyond my control.

At that time, my faith in God was shaky. It was almost nonexistent. Society and circumstances had indeed taken a toll on me. I was angry with God. Why on earth would you leave me here to suffer? It just didn't add up. That's when I decided to put him to the test. First of all, who am I to tell God he needed to show me that he was real. For those who are believers, I know you are looking at me sideways, but I know I am not the only one who had been at such a low point to where questioning God was the only thing that made sense. I just needed answers. I wanted relief.

My God, My God! Let me tell you when they say he will never leave you nor forsake you. Man. He isn't always there when you want him, but he is always on time!! Somebody say, "AMEN!"

God created a definite shift in our marriage. It was almost instant. I asked my husband to attend a private bible study with me, and to my surprise, he said yes. I said surprise because before that moment he said that he wasn't interested. We went to bible study for a few weeks, and eventually, we both were baptized. You see, he made room for understanding and to even out the fight. But he left us both with the task to work through the kinks on our own. Once again, I didn't know what working through things looked like, but I began to try. Sometimes the slightest change can ignite a flame in a dark place, no matter the size.

I realized that all that time, I was fighting the wrong fight. Instead of fighting for my marriage, I needed to be fighting for the love I had for myself. I hadn't poured into myself. I was still carrying so much self-doubt, insecurities, and fear. You never understand the importance of fixing yourself until it hinders you from excelling in life. Sure, many outside factors hold people back, which caused the damage that needs fixing in the first place. The fact remains that somebody has to fix it, so why not start with you.

Like Santa Claus, I made a list of all the good and bad in my life. My goal was to improve and remove. So the work began. The funny thing about this process was that the more I improved the good, the bad just removed itself naturally. As we grow, most things and people that are not for us just seem not to fit, and organically they fade away. Pay attention. I said most, not all—some stuff you have to throw out and cut off manually. I used to feel some sort of guilt for getting rid of all that was toxic. But that stems from not being free; at that point, I was free-ish.

From my weight to my career, I began to improve. Somewhere along that ride, by forcing myself to say affirmations and write down moments that made me feel low, I started gaining clarity. That clarity opened my eyes to see the beautiful and ugly truths about myself. That clarity forced me to accept myself for who I was at that moment. That clarity gave me the space to rebuild and reshape the pieces of me.

Looking back on situations where people would label me or call out my character, I would get so angry. I mean, no one has the right to tell me who they think I am. In the back of my mind, some part of me knew they were right. I didn't want to believe I was messed up in so many ways. But I was.

I would be lying if I said this process took a month. It took me two years to get here from the time I started to revamp my existence. Not only did I have to look at myself, but I also had to look at what factors played a role in the woman I used to be. I didn't want to face them because then it would mean that people deliberately caused me pain, it meant I accepted things I shouldn't have, and I had played a part in my stagnation. But the facts are the facts, no matter how you choose to receive them.

All in all, the struggles in my marriage gave me the courage to fight. I was fighting for something real. However, that fight was never supposed to be the biggest fight of my life, as I tried to make it. It was the fight that prepared me for the actual battle. Battling self-doubt, lack of self-worth, the inability to see my purpose, was an important phase in my life. I needed that pain to awake the warrior in me. That pain led me to self-love. That self-love gave me the true grit that it takes to love others. Love - with all its power, rid my life of unnecessary negativity that held me hostage and slowed my process.

But a good friend of mine said something to me that let me know that it was okay that I wasn't exactly where I wanted to be and that there is always a greater later. She said, "Sometimes we are delayed but never denied." Don't tell her I am admitting this, but boy am I happy that she was right.

III. Awakening

Chapter 4

Forgive Yourself

"Relax. Don't be so hard on yourself. You are living and learning. Forgive yourself and grow from the experience."

Mood

Open Your Eyes - John Legend
Love Yourz - J. Cole
Hate on Me - Jill Scott
The Climb - Miley Cyrus

Let the record show that this will be the only moment during our journey together that I speak about my ex. Anywho, my ex-boyfriend was the true definition of a womanizer. Ya'll, I am so embarrassed that I let a dude who openly admitted he was in resource classes during grade school and who failed out of college play me like a fool. Now before you puff out your chest, I am in no way talking down on kids who are in resource classes. Hell, I taught Special Education for almost a full school year.

I am simply saying that as a smart young woman, I should have noticed my self-worth and walked away from his foolishness the moment he played the game raw.

Of course, I was young, dumb, and in love. I was also shallow. I was a volleyball player, and he played basketball, so he fit into my image of what I thought I wanted. Nonetheless, he broke me all the way down. I was a fine little something when he met me, and a full-grown walrus when I finally found the strength to leave. Never again, I can promise you that.

Now before we get into the nitty-gritty, let me make this disclaimer, because I know some of you are going to be like now waymentttt sis, I didn't see this before. Be that as it may, you did see many different things in my life that caused me pain, and although I didn't mention this healing method, just know it was there, and this is where it came to life.

Okay, we good? Roll playbackkkkk.

When I decided to leave my ex, I truly believed I was done. I was firm in my departure, firm that it was over and firm that he wasn't meant for me. I made sure that he knew I forgave him for all that he had done. Not that he deserved it. I forgave him because I was numb to him, and he no longer had access to my heart. I forgave him because I hoped that it would show that he no longer impacted me, that he had missed out and that he could now free himself from guilt. After all, I had pardoned him.

Forgiveness is a powerful thing. It's necessary to move on and grow. But forgiving someone verbally doesn't always completely rid us of the pain at that moment. Where it may mask the feeling, it doesn't always wash them away. Nevertheless, after that day, I went on about my life feeling brand new and ready to see what else was out there. I mean, at this pointtttt, what did I have to lose!

Let's fast forward to the summer I started spending time with my now-husband. He was truly a breath of fresh air. He was always smiling, always happy, and always looking at things in its best light. To be honest, he was too damn happy, and it made me mad. Sometimes his happiness was downright annoying, and I would find a reason to try to dim his light. Who does that? You mean to tell me I was so miserable that I would deliberately try to dim someone's light just because I was in the dark.

Yep. I did that.

I guess he grew tired of my bullshit because next thing I knew, he hit me with the, "maybe we should just be friends" text.

Now for all my fellas who are reading this, that text is equivalent to the "I think we need to talk" text. It stops you in your tracks and makes you recap what sparked the text in the first place. But I didn't have to wonder why he sent it. He told me that I was too angry and unless I could release that anger, he didn't see this working out.

Listennnnnnnnnnnn when I say this, I was shook!

At first, I thought, how dare him. He must not know I am a prize. But that's the issue. He knew I was something worth keeping. He just couldn't take on that negative energy.

I remember panicking because I didn't know when that timeline to get rid of my anger would lapse. So I did what most people do when they think they are sick. I google-searched ways to release anger. I'm not exaggerating, I went straight to google and started looking for an answer. I mean, I had no one to ask. I couldn't ask my mom because she dwelled in anger. I couldn't ask my brother because I was his human google search so what could he possibly tell me and I couldn't ask my friends because most were so exhausted with the thought of my ex, I didn't want to bother them. So, Google was my best friend.

Surprisingly, google came through for your girl.

Cues music - And I'm forever indebted, and I'm forever indebted.

I know we don't fool with R. Kelly, but that's literally how I felt.

While most of the stuff I came across was directing me to meditate, do yoga or exercise, all of which I wasn't even in shape to do, I did find one gem. This particular article, of which I honestly can't remember the name or who wrote it, spoke about forgiveness. At first glance, I assumed it would guide me in ways to forgive the person that wronged me, but that wasn't the case. The article simply said that to relieve yourself of pain, one must forgive themselves for allowing it to happen to them in the first place.

Instantly, I was like clearly the author is stupid. Why would anyone blame themselves for the pain that someone else caused? Yet, I kept reading. I'm glad I kept reading because I don't know what life would be like had I stopped. You know the saying that people only do what you allow? Well, it couldn't be more accurate. The article went in-depth about how often the hurt we experience from others is due to us allowing it to happen. Of course, there are several instances where that doesn't apply, but, in this scenario, it hit the nail on its head.

I had allowed myself to get hurt. I ignored several signs and chose to extend more chances, even when I knew better. I am infamous for saying, "If you knew better, you would do better. But you didn't." As I wrote that just now, I burst out laughing. If someone paid me a dollar every time that I said that I'd be driving that Bentayga already. I'm laughing even harder because I just realized I used to love a good saying that portrayed confidence and I had none. But I told ya'll I was once a perpetrator.

So, there I sat, angry that I had allowed someone to make me angry. I cried and cried. But crying wouldn't fix me. It was time to come up with an action plan. So, I did. I wrote out all the things my ex did to hurt me and then wrote all the ways I allowed it to continue. Once I finished, I went to the mirror and started reading them out loud one by one. With each one, I ended the statement by saying, "I forgive me." It was therapeutic. It was painful. And at that moment, it set me free.

After that, I hung out with my husband again. I didn't tell him what I had done, nor did I bring attention to the anger he once noticed. I guess he saw the shift in my behavior or maybe not. Either way, it helped me, and seven years later, we are now husband and wife.

So apparently the shit worked.

It's Levels To This Shit

Remember when I said the forgiveness tactic worked? Well, let's just say it became an old faithful. Old faithful's are all good until it gets overused and loses its impact. It lowkey becomes useless.

Apparently, behind the anger I had, there was old pinned up anger. Even more so, after moving past that patch of darkness, I was headed into an even bigger trail of trauma. Go figure. Hell, ya'll read about my childhood, what did you expect? Of course, several moments in my life caused this new anger. And even my forgiveness was not powerful enough to sever the ties that held my soul hostage.

As a little girl, I had a specific vision for my dream wedding day. As I grew older, my vision only got bigger. The wedding would be big, my dress would be mermaid style, I would have eight bridesmaids, my first dance song would be 'Spend My Life My Life With You,' my father-daughter dance would be epic, and my future husband would tear up when I came down the aisle. I just knew that I would go wedding dress shopping with my bride tribe and mom. I'd act like a bridezilla, and they all would cry when I said Yes to the Dress! On my wedding day, you would feel the love and be overwhelmed by a room full of my closest family and friends who would be so happy to see me marry the man of my dreams.

Sounds lovely, right? Sounds like a day to remember; it sounds like a dream. It would be too much like right if all dreams come true.

It was about two weeks before my wedding day. Things had been a little rocky between my soon to be husband and me. We had completed marriage counseling, which was tough. He and I truly didn't argue about much, but there was one thing that could start a full-blown war between us in less than 60 seconds.

Does anyone want to take a crack at what was so destructive that it could declare war? Anybody? If your answer was my family, then please move past go, collect two hundred dollars as you head to your next destination.

My family had banned together and decided they weren't coming to my wedding. Every time I think about this episode, I feel my blood boil, so bear with me. My mom dropped me off at my house one day. I wasn't able to drive due to the seizure after giving birth to my firstborn. As we arrive at my house, my aunt pulls up. My mom and aunt start talking about the baby, so I proceed to get out of the car. I guess I missed the part where my mom invited my aunt into my house. To be clear, my mom does not live at my house. So, it wasn't her place to invite her in. Yet, as I opened my front door, my aunt and mom just waltz right on in. Mind you, my son was asleep, and my husband was in pajamas. Here is where a whole load of drama comes in. My mom looked at my husband and said hello. And this dude looks her dead in her eyes and utters not one word back. She repeated her hello, and he continued to stare at her until she left out the door.

Listen! One thing you should know about my husband is that anything that disturbs me, or his household is the enemy. Ask anyone who was on the receiving end of his wrath. If you mistreated me or disrespected the home team in any shape or form, just know he is coming behind us like an army. So, his actions towards my mom in that instance were of no shock to me.

Within two hours, my phone was ringing off the hook. Voicemails and text messages expressing deep disappointment in me. How could I let him disrespect my mom like that? That was the common message amongst the collective.

So, let's get this straight. She invited not only herself but another person into his house that she didn't have permission to occupy, and when he reacted in disapproval, he got deemed disrespectful. Oh okay.

All my life, I was taught that if my mom felt some type of way by the actions of someone else, then that person must be wrong. But he wasn't wrong, and I knew it. Yet that didn't stop me from feeling conflicted. My mind wanted to be covered with wool. I started trying to get him to apologize to her. I even convinced myself that he had disrespected her while at the same time telling my family that I don't see the disrespect. That's twisted as hell.

This went on for days. This next part took me out ya'll. My mom and granny came over like four days before my wedding. On the cool, I think they were trying to conduct an intervention. They sat me down and argued their case as to why I shouldn't marry this man. Even after they admitted that although they didn't like the fact that he didn't acknowledge my mom, his actions weren't disrespectful, they still kept at it. One thing that my mom and granny always say that has to be one of the dumbest things I've heard in my life, but still they say it with so much confidence. My granny looked at me and said, "I know that you are about to become one and are supposed to submit to your husband, but God also gave you five senses." Say what now? I know you fucking lying! Whew, I'm dead! I can't make this stuff up. Like what does that even mean? If that's all ya'll got, then I may just marry him tonight. But they both took it a step further and asked if I was insecure or desperate. They wanted me to feel low and needy. If I choose him, then that lowness and neediness was a sign of weakness. If I chose them, then those same characteristics were justified because we are family and have each other's back. What in the American Horror Story is this mess I call my life?

We get to the day before the wedding, and my granny calls me. She asked me what I was doing, so I replied, "I'm about to head to the hotel in Austin to meet up with my friends for my last night of freedom." This woman said, "So you still getting married tomorrow? I figured you were going to call it off." Her reply was not funny then, but now I'm crying laughing! I mean, they were hell-bent on me changing my mind.

Well, we made it to my wedding day, and I guess they had to make one final attempt. My mom woke me up early to look at the venue since I had never seen it. We get there, and she goes on and on about how bad it seems. When it was time to put on my dress and take pre-down the aisle photos and video footage, she demanded they wait until she got dressed. I only had a one and half hour time slot at the venue. Let us not forget that she left the rings in the room as I was walking up the path towards the aisle. They had to pause my introduction music so that they could get them.

Are you starting to see the trend?

They didn't even want to be there. My family didn't smile nor cry. It was so fake. At the reception, the foolery continued. My husband was furious, and I was scarred.

This was so far from what I imagined. What made it worse was I had to settle for a quick small wedding because my entire family refused to give me a wedding if I was going to marry my husband. So, you robbed me of my fairytale, and you deliberately ruined my wedding day. The thought that they could be so selfish destroyed me.

Instead of a dream, I was experiencing a nightmare. If you look at my wedding video, you will think it was a real loving, intimate wedding. That wasn't the case. But I appreciate my videographer for his excellent storytelling skills. He definitely deserved more than what I paid him.

Even after all of that, my dumb ass forgave them. I consistently tried to get my husband to conform to their norms and make him think that his perspective was off. I tried to convince him to coexist with them and come with me to family events. I was brainwashed. I mean, that's the only rational reason someone would give the culprits another chance to access their life.

I was still lost in the sauce. I forgave myself for allowing them to taint my mind. But what does forgiving myself do for me if I know nothing is going to change? It was like playing the same depressing song on repeat. It's insanity, and it ruined the meaning of forgiveness.

So Meek Mill was right when he said it's levels to this shit. I had reached the highest level of denial, and the act of forgiveness, no matter the recipient, wasn't strong enough. And while it's a great tool, it's irrelevant if no change is going to come.

Never Again

Forgive and forget has become a statement that people tend to bend to appease their sense of self. For a long time, I would say it in a way that meant I'll forgive a person but not forget that it happened. I used the forget portion as a bookmark. I wanted to put a placeholder on the moment, to keep a record of the wrongdoing. I tried to keep tally so that I could remind myself that I was a great person and the other person was lucky to have me in their life. Knowing that more wrong was being done to me, then the wrong I put out, was oddly satisfying. But I wasn't satisfied. I was just building a platform for excuses.

There are two methods of forgiveness. Forgiving others and forgiving yourself.

I will start with forgiving others. Forgiving someone is a big deal, so don't let anyone downplay the power that is attached to that action. It is not only a release. It serves as a milestone. That milestone can look different depending on your perspective. I will say that if you forgive someone just to place yourself in a superior seat, you won't truly move past the pain, you will have only put a lid on it until it serves you as ammunition. Here is how that situation plays out. One person does something horrible to the other person, leaving one person in the position to forgive and the other to be forgiven. So, the one who does the forgiving adds that moment to their stash of wins, and then in a moment when they need to manipulate a situation in their favor, they resurface that moment to bring that old issue up to have the upper hand. So not only is this person going tit for tat, but they are also plungy, always bringing up old shit. Nobody likes the smell of shit, so let's agree to flush all that.

Forgiving others is only effective if you are genuinely ready to move past the situation. It works best when you realize that forgiving them is not to massage their feelings but to release you from the hurt their actions caused. What I realized over time was, when I forgave others to make them feel less terrible for what they had done to me, nine times out of ten, they would do it again. That tells me two things, they were never sorry and that it's just who they truly are as a person. To avoid the room for disappointment, I chose to start forgiving people to create separation of my soul from the power that hurt had over me. They didn't deserve to have that much impact on my wellbeing.

Next, let's work through this forgiving ourselves portion. At first, this was extremely hard to do. It always felt like I was blaming myself for allowing someone else to hurt me. Essentially, when you forgive yourself, you are telling yourself that you played a role in the pain you feel. But it isn't in the form of blame. It's more so in the way of accepting that you could have cut it off sooner, while at the same time giving yourself a break, being that no one deliberately wants to be mistreated.

Breaking down each scenario is the hardest part. During that breakdown, you'll start to reveal some patterns. You will see common weaknesses and triggers that are ignored. This caused me to think about why I didn't find the signs alarming. In my lifetime, I faced several situations that exposed some ugly truths about my upbringing. I found out that threats of physical harm didn't scare me. In my head, monogamy was unrealistic for men, promises are expected to be broken, and money somehow equates to the depth of someone's love. So, if anything happened within the realm of what I presumed to be normal, then it never made me raise an eyebrow. I guess it would cause me to be blind to the fires in front of me. Blind until I felt the burn.

Thankfully, out of the darkness, forgiving myself forced me to start seeing the light. The process gave me insight into the way I moved through life and a perspective into why people cause and accept pain. I would be lying to say that I now know all signs and successfully avoid all pain. That just wouldn't be truthful. But what I can say is that I try my best not to experience the same hurt by the same things repeatedly.

Which brings me to the golden rule. I want you all to hear me, so please get your pen and paper out. While we practice the art of forgiveness in all of its glory, please remember that you should never forget what brought you to that moment. Further, you should never forget the person behind the action because while they may mask their behavior, they likely have not changed. So, I like to say forgive but never forget, and that is necessary. Even so, I want you to know that it is great to forgive and not forget, but you should definitely forget the person behind the act. They are toxic. They are not team you, and they will definitely hold you back.

Someone recently asked me, "What could a person (mainly a family member) do so bad to cause you to want to exile them? Outside of something harmful to you physically, what could be so bad?" I looked that person in the eye and said, "You know how we see so many suicides and wonder why would someone want to kill themselves, saying things like 'it never gets that bad,' well though I have never gotten to that low point, some people do, and that often comes from emotional pain and pinned up mental trauma." The mind is the devil's playground. No one should have to keep a person around or interact with someone who negatively invades their mental state, just because of the proximity of the relationship. That is ludicrous.

When it comes to family, we don't have a say or choice as to who they are when we are brought into this world. As we grow older, we have more of a say as to what and who we consider family, regardless of the blood that runs through our veins. In most cases, half the people that we call aunt and uncle, or cousin aren't truly our blood relatives, but I am not even about to discuss that tea today. Anyway, family doesn't mean we have to accept bullshit.

I have figured out who is for me and who isn't. I have forgotten some completely, and some I've placed limitations on their access to my life. I call it out of sight, out of mind. Once I realized that those people trigger me, I started to phase them out. It wasn't deliberate or intentional. It just naturally happened. It seemed that once my mind had an epiphany, then it started ridding me of the need to give that toxicity any rise or energy. So, I started to move differently. Moves that pissed many off, while at the same time showed me those who were cheering me on.

Craziest part of it all is that I could care less who is mad, who disapproves and who may feel the need to tear me down. I remember watching Vampire Diaries, and each time one of the vampires experienced some kind of mental turn point, they would turn their humanity off and become relentless. Well, I haven't turned off my humanity, but I did turn my pleasing others switch off and turned on my relentless pursuit to be the best me. I expected that many wouldn't like the woman I have become, but then I remember hell they didn't like the woman I was before. Beggars can't be choosers. They will be alright.

So, let's reflect a bit. It is perfectly okay to forgive others, forgive yourself, and move on. Additionally, it is important to not only never forget the things that brought you to that forgiveness, but you have every right to forget the person behind the actions. You don't have to explain your decisions nor ask permission. The overall mission is that you are at peace with you. That when the storm is over, and all is quiet. You can sit back and say, "damn what a storm, but I am grateful it's over."

Chapter 5

Highest In The Room

"I am worthy of great praise, I am worthy of happiness, I am worthy to live a life full of joy."

Mood

24K Magic - Bruno Mars
Sorry Not Sorry - Demi Lovato
Highest In The Room - Travis Scott

I've been called annoying more than enough. Actually, quite often, to be honest. Crazy thing is, I wear that term as a badge of honor. One thing about being annoying is that you make a mark on others, whether they accept it or not. When I want something, I stop at nothing to reach my goal. There is a saying that the worst someone can say to you is no. Apparently, my interpretation of that saying is wrong because when someone says "no," all I hear is "not yet." So, I continue to press and push towards everything I see for myself. Persistence is what it's called, and though people may be agitated, they will remember you.

What I realized throughout my career, is that when a man pushes and pushes, he is seen as eager and driven. It is applauded, placed on a pedestal of some sort as if he is doing something so brave. But let a woman act in the same manner, she is seen as pushy and desperate. It is frowned upon because they aren't supposed to be aggressive or forward. There is no trophy to reward a woman's effort; in most cases, there is some sort of reprimand for the "unheard" of behavior. A bubble was built around our place in this world, and how dare we bust through its boundaries. Well, guess what? If they didn't want women to break through the surface, they should've built a stronger barrier.

Women tend to allow society to shape their worth. We tend to accept being second to men without noticing. And we certainly fall victim to "staying in our lane." To be honest, I call it bullshit. I got so sick and tired of accepting the "norm" that I decided to go rogue. But before I went off the rails, I was completely stuck. I allowed others to keep me in a place that lacked risk. Those people are complacent and project their fears onto you. Those people are one track-minded and can't see past their views. Those people are HATERS, and we need to call it like we see it.

That collective pack that I call haters consisted of both men and women. Some were family members, and some were "friends." What I learned from that pack is that they will only encourage you up to the ceiling they set for themselves. This ceiling will be no higher than their reach and will not give you the room to grow past the level that serves them. The worst part about this ceiling is that it is presented in a manner that gives you a sliver of hope that you are working towards your potential. In reality, it is likely the floor of your potential, and the person who built it wants to keep you grounded. I'll expand on that point.

So, this pack of people is hard to spot or point out when you haven't expanded your mind to see your path to tap into your potential. This group of people may not even know that they are the problem. So, don't expect any of them to slow down their hateration, as Mary J Blige calls it, because they don't even know they are doing it. But let's all hope that one day they become aware of their ways for everyone's sake.

After graduating from law school, I worked several jobs. None of which ever lasted a full year. I blamed the jobs, my circumstances, and even my decision to go to law school. But I realized it was some of those things, yet there was more depth to it. The truth is I kept looking at other people's success, and it made me wonder why I can't be where they are. I measured success based on someone else's journey. I looked at so many teachers, nurses, and many others who hadn't obtained a masters or doctorate and wondered how they were able to go on so many trips, buy luxury cars, and expensive designer clothes. I was so confused because they were thriving. I never stopped to gain insight into their circumstances or priorities. Quite frankly, that was not my damn business. Like, why was I so pressed at what they had going on? I will admit that I wanted what they had. I was envious and jealous all at the same time. Now while I wanted what they had, let's not confuse the facts, your girl may have been jealous, but I was never a hater.

So, there I was, continuously choosing jobs that undervalued me just because they matched my educational background. I know someone out there is wondering why a person would willingly settle for that. The simple answer is we accept mediocrity because our systematic mindset tells us, it's "what we are supposed to do." The worst part of it all is that when you find yourself in this situation, you have already lost. You are indeed already ten steps behind and likely have no method to change your direction.

It didn't help that I kept taking the bar exam over and over, listening to my family and friends who felt that it was the end all be all to reach success. Did you catch that? I put myself through rigorous months of studying to chase a dream that I never even dreamed of. I kept settling for enough to survive instead of fulfilling the happiness I yearned. This isn't uncommon, I mean we all want happiness in our careers, but when you find yourself between a rock and a hard place, you don't see how happiness plays a role in how your bills are paid. Well, let me tell you happiness is a factor towards the greater later, just keep reading.

One day I found myself looking at the profile of people that I envied. They came from all walks of life, some were my former law school classmates who were now barred attorneys, and others were people I knew from other times in life who were entrepreneurs. What struck me was that they all had one thing in common. The common ground that jumped out at me was that they all were happy. I know many people have a knack for portraying happiness when they aren't truly happy. But this wasn't that. These people displayed a level of joy that jumped out at you. That's when I realized that I was not happy. I hadn't tapped into what ignites my soul, and until I did, I would always be on the outside looking through the looking glass, an outsider to my greatness. That couldn't be my life. Something had to shake. And it needed to shake expeditiously.

Thereupon, I began to think, what will it take to live the life I want? I told myself that I would find what brings me a joy that I can't explain. I searched and searched. But what was I searching for? Certainly, the answer wasn't on google. The answer was inside me. I started to think about all the topics of conversations I had with people that sparked my brain. I started thinking back on the things I had done in the life that filled me. That's when I realized that whatever path I took, I wanted to be able to leverage my legal knowledge to make changes in others' lives. Still, I didn't know exactly what that job or career path should be, but I knew it would be to serve others the best way I could.

As I mentioned before, after Hurricane Harvey, I accepted a position with the SBA. The work was tedious, and unlike they described, it didn't truly utilize my legal knowledge. But what that position did give me was the opportunity to impact so many lives. I'm talking thousands of lives. I was a part of something bigger than myself. It was a position that taught me sacrifice. A sacrifice that was necessary to serve those in need. Unfortunately, this job was one of those jobs that wouldn't last a year. So, I had to figure out how to continue my calling to serve others. I started applying to other jobs. I kept being denied positions because I simply was too much or not enough. I was given opportunities but told that I was only good enough to be at entry-level. It seemed that I would approach several tables, but the seats were full. There was no room for what I had to offer.

I even decided to pursue teaching, thinking that it would be awesome to start with the youth. Also, no offense, but there is such a shortage for teachers due to the low pay rate, that they were accepting almost anyone. I accepted a full-time special education and head volleyball coaching position. I figured I would get to help our youth and pour into them, which is serving others, so this could be where I am needed. But what I ran into was more barriers and restrictions. I didn't go through all those years of school and accumulate that much student loan debt to be told once again to stay in my lane. No ma'am, Pam. Babyyyyyyyyyyyy, let's just say that's going to be a NO for me. I love the kids and respect teachers, but I was meant to do more.

I was three months pregnant, experiencing extreme nausea, with plenty of time to think. My husband was supportive of whatever move I decided to make. So that was my green light. And guess what your girl did?

Yepppppp, I quit!

I dabbled in real estate during my pregnancy. Once again, I figured I could help others and also figure out what is meant for me. I spent months chasing clients, doing open houses, and showings for other agents. But not one dollar was made. This made me remember why I never desired to be an attorney. I never wanted to have to chase people down for money. PERIOD. It was not me. I didn't like that so much I went back to the idea of teaching and secured another teaching position that I would start after coming off maternity leave. Well, it came time for me to have my baby, so of course, that put a pause on everything. I had my second son, and it was like his existence made easier to see a need to find my true calling. I don't know if it was the pressure that I needed to help provide, the need for stability or that just surviving wasn't going to cut it. All I know is that my outlook on what I wanted for my family, mostly what I wanted for myself, had changed. Just like that, the shift began.

My oldest son wasn't fully potty trained, so I started working with him. We decided to send him to a local daycare to get more help. My son is brilliant, so the classwork was never an issue. Most of his teachers bragged about his level of knowledge. But not this daycare. That was not their concern. He was a nuisance because he didn't know how to go to the restroom properly. They even tried to be slick and keep him in a classroom that was beneath his age range so that they didn't have to deal with him. Earlier I spoke about how my outlook on what I saw for my family changed, well that included my kids.

The time was getting closer for me to start working at the new school, meaning my infant would be attending daycare. I tried to talk myself into letting him start, but I couldn't do it. No money, no pressure or need to survive was worth sending my kids into a situation that could set them back for years. I wanted better for them, and I knew that to give them better, I had to do better. It was time that I laid the notion that by any means meant accepting crumbs, to rest. My husband and I talked, and he spoke so much life into me. He said, "You worked so hard for your degree, you have accomplished so much, you put your dreams on hold to be a mother, to support me in my endeavors, but now it is your time. I don't want to hear about any more jobs that offer you a position if it isn't something that acknowledges your worth or doesn't make you happy. Like, don't even tell me about it. When you find what truly makes you happy at that moment, I will entertain a conversation on our next move. But until then, don't present it." It never fails that he knows exactly what to say to get me all the way together. So, the next day, I wrote my letter of resignation to the school that I was to start teaching and began to seek better.

Politics was always something that I tapped into, but the idea of actually diving into it seemed so far out of reach. I started applying for positions with different campaigns. I also began an internship with a powerful woman in politics, so I could reactivate my legal knowledge and see where it can be handy in the political arena. Finally, I started getting interviews with some of the campaigns, and offers were made. But I didn't want to move. I applied for one position that offered me the ability to be remote and tap into my skills. It wasn't a position that utilized all of my skills, but it was my way in. It was my turning point. So shoutout to my former boss and now friend for seeing something in me during a time that you didn't even know was a much-needed transition period for my life.

During my time on the campaign trail, I traveled more often than none. Talk about a real sacrifice for my family to help me while I pursued my dreams. I will always cherish that because they didn't have to do that. But luckily, they did because that experience changed my life.

On the trail, I started seeing how much power I had behind my thoughts. I started seeing my impact, and I started noticing that years of experience didn't matter. I found myself being the smartest in the room, even amongst those who were my superiors. They had years, but they had low expectations. I was a quick learner, I was an innovator, and I wasn't settling for just enough. So many men on the trail would try to limit me and keep me in the position that best served their interests. But they didn't know what they had done. Hell, I didn't know what they had done yet, but it would soon surface.

In addition to the men on the trail trying to hold me back, I still had a small hand in real estate. I still wanted to fit it in. The broker that I was with charged us with the task of doing four hours of office hours throughout the month to hold ourselves accountable. Well, that's at least how he presented it. It was not mandatory, but boy did it sure feel like it was. He would watch me travel and post about the campaign on my social media, so he knew when I was in town. But mostly, it was as if he was keeping tabs. He wrote to me one day and said that he knows I travel, but when I come back, I have time for real estate. I told him when I am home. I work from home. Not to mention, I am a whole wife and mother, so any time that I have free, it goes to them. His response was something I will never forget because, at that moment, my mindset changed forever. This dude said to me in so many words that he gets that I am a mother and all but that I am not the only person that has kids and is busy. He said that I didn't know what hard work or hustle looked like because if I did, I would be in the office. As I started to type back that he had me all wrong, I realized I don't owe him an explanation, nor do I need to prove to him that I could work hard. Once again, another man was trying to place a limit or expectation on my potential. Another man, who, while is very successful, doesn't even have the mindset nor credentials to sit at my table. So back the fuck up and go about your business. As the young folk says, "mind the business that pays you," and we will all be just fine.

Whew chile, I just got pissed off real quick. He trieddddddddd it.

But that moment did something to me. It shook my spirit. My mind started racing. I was fed up. The trend of letting other people, specifically men, dictate my worth had run its course. That's when it hit me. GIRL, YOU ARE THE SHIT, grab a chair and pull right on up to that table! If you can't find a seat, become the got damn table! From that moment, I told myself if there isn't room, I'll become the space!! I felt like I had taken a limitless pill or something because you couldn't tell me shit after that.

I stopped letting job descriptions stop me from applying. Honestly, I don't even read the required qualifications portion. When I see a job that describes what I know I can do, I just apply. If my resume doesn't match up, you're still gonna get this light. I landed a new job right after the campaign, which still involved politics. It was something new, and I felt useful. Yet, I found myself still feeling diminished. I hadn't become the table. I had only accepted a seat.

They saw my worth, but when you work for others, you still are placed in a box. It just isn't enough.

So how does someone make space? How do you become more visible? How do you insert yourself and say, "look no further, I'm what you've been looking for?" First, you stop presenting yourself to others to fit into their needs. Second, you find a problem and become the solution. I decided that if I work for anyone, it will be a choice. It will be allowing them to be lucky enough to share my excellence. Finally, I decided that I would start a business of my own that allowed me to do what I love and play by my own rules. Now you don't have to be your own boss to become the table. You just have to make sure that others know that having you is the greatest thing that happened to them, while at the same time not letting them use you.

Face it. People will use you for their benefit. But that doesn't mean you can't benefit at the same time. A key component is that your benefit from the interaction is far greater than the pieces of you that you share. Finally, always remember you are the table, so if they want access or a seat, they better make it worth your time. We get one life, one chance to build a table we can be proud of and one lifetime to create something to pass down for generations to come. So, make it count.

Assuming Responsibility

When I'm dead and gone, I often wonder what the legacy of my existence will be. If and when I reached the level of success that I saw for myself, will it all have been worth it? I mean, of course, my kids will reap the reward of my hard work. They will likely be left with money to set them up for a lifetime. Of course, that is the ultimate goal. But what does that do for my true purpose to impact and serve others? If my children are the only ones to benefit from my life's work, then have I truly fulfilled what I was placed on this earth to achieve? In my eyes, if that is the outcome, then I only accomplished half of my life's mission.

My former boss used to drop serious gems on me when it came to what makes someone a true leader. I always knew I could lead. I had led in a number of my previous positions, but it wasn't effective. In our interview, he made the point to say that it is his goal to hire individuals that he believes he could grow and give guidance to lead them into the next level of their potential. In fact, he had already had a plan on exactly how he would make that happen. I was amazed by that. No one throughout my career found it necessary to push my purpose, to shine light on my potential, or even take the time to offer guidance. But he was different. He led without being a dictator. He gave room for me to share in leadership and accepted my input with open arms. You see, he knew that he didn't have the answers to all the questions and that he had room to learn from others.

He was humble. He knew what he knew and what he didn't know.

We were very similar. We both believed in professionalism, organization, and attention to detail. We were very meticulous. We both were open to expanding our knowledge and seek things that kept us on our toes. It was through those similarities that we had to learn to accept that we were exceptional at many things outside of the task we were employed to do.

Through our interactions, I learned something valuable from him. I learned that leadership comes with a lot of baggage. He used to always talk about how, when you reach a level where you now have a seat at the table, you are burdened with more, more meetings, and a load of hard decisions. Amongst that baggage, he would tell me how one portion is not a burden but a real obligation. That obligation is that when you make it to a level of success or leadership, you must assume the responsibility to bring others up with you. He didn't ever really speak to how to act on this obligation. He just made sure that I knew that leadership contained much more than a seat at the table.

I had never thought about that aspect of leadership or success. I always thought that if I reach a certain level of success, it would be an automatic reaction that others would follow in my footsteps. But that's the thing. You don't lead in hopes of gaining more followers. You lead to develop more leaders. I mean, let's look at it. What good does it do for a person who strives to invoke change or make an impact on others, only to attract a herd of people that will only follow them? Change, in most cases, starts with one person but usually is executed with many like minds who have the same access. To have equal access, a leader needs to help create more leaders. They say it takes a village to raise children, well that can be found true when seeking to make an economic change.

There is nothing wrong with being a follower. I believe that most who become leaders had to learn how to follow at some point in time. Follow does not mean fall behind; we must know the difference. But it is not just enough to follow. You have to follow effectively.

During college, a professor once told me that I paid for my education, so it is my right to make my professors earn their pay. It is no different in a work setting. In any job that I obtained, I make it my business to ask a ton of questions and pick leadership's brain. They were placed in that position to lead, guide, and teach, so who am I to derail their duties? Therefore, to be an effective follower, you have to make room to learn.

Further, you have to enhance your skills through the knowledge you gain and find a way to implement that into your growth. As for me, in every situation, I challenged myself to learn everything about my position and my supervisor's position within the first 30-60 days. I didn't do that to take their spot or squeeze past them. I did it to show how quickly I adapt and learn because I did not want to fall behind. When a person shows that they are content, never challenges their superior to teach them, and sits back waiting for someone to see what they can do, they almost always get left behind. I never wanted to be amongst the forgotten. So, I played my part, and when given the small space to grab the steering wheel to advance, I smashed my foot on the gas and flew past those beside me. Once you recognize that you were destined to lead, you no longer let others determine your destination.

Before I became a true leader, I used to speak on other leaders and share my disappointment that they had chosen to be greedy by shutting others out. We often see many people who appear selfish when they get to the so-called top. Thinking they must've forgotten where they came from is how the old saying goes. But it isn't always the case. It is important that once you begin on the journey of creating more leaders, you must have discernment. Everyone can't come. I say that because you will meet many people who have potential and need room to grow. Those people will learn from you, push their potential, and excel in their real purpose. In the same breath, you will meet many leeches. They will suck the life out of you and attach themselves to your success, feeding off of your greatness while benefiting significantly off of your mere existence. That is where discernment is necessary. You have to see the difference quickly. It isn't easy, but over time you will learn to have an eye for it.

It is a tough position, to be honest. The responsibility gets tiresome at times. The obligation comes with the role of being the life speaker and encourager. I was once a person who couldn't see my potential. I'm certain people were sick of me in the past. But I am happy that some never gave up on me. Even when they were exhausted by my inability to see the person that I was meant to be, they kept pushing. Their dedication to bringing me up is admirable. It is because of them that I can see both sides of the road. Now, as I am in the position to lead, I try my best not to get frustrated with those that I help. They are the depiction of the woman I used to be, and I know that if I can get them to see what awaits them, they will go on to do great things.

Take the time to understand that leadership in itself is hard to step into. It's even harder to lead with purpose. Recognizing that leadership is more than making it to the top and bigger than showing others that they didn't hold you back. Leadership is a reward and a position to share your playbook with others so that they can create their own and pay it forward.

Reach one, Teach one, right? I challenge you to not only make a difference in someone's life but be truly instrumental in their path to success. Without a doubt, it has made me a better person, and I hope it has the same effect on you.

IV. Arrival

Chapter 6

Silence Speaks Volumes

"If you wanna fly, you got to give up the shit that weighs you down." - Toni Morrison

Mood

Champion - Kanye West
Sorry Not Sorry - Demi Lovato
Ballin' - Mustard ft. Roddy Ricch

Ever met a "me too" type of person? The person that always has to let it be known that they have done what you plan to do or has been to a place where you intend to visit. The person that is always right and has to win every game. I call those people the "one uppers." Well, I have met several that fit that description. Sometimes I would make up something outrageous that I wanted to do, just to see if they would say they had done that in the past. Now you and I both know they always said they did. Most times, it would seriously tickle me, but in other instances, I found the need to call their bluff or bring them down to size. It irked my nerves so bad having to listen to that mess. So, of course, I had to be the one to burst their bubble. I don't know why I felt the need to make sure they knew that they were doing the most or wrong. I guess I thought I was the layer of truth. But I wasn't the layer of truth. I just needed to level the playing field. Still, it was a waste of energy.

One of my former classmates once said to me, "If someone thinks that they are the best actor alive, then just let them think that.' He encouraged me to root for them like, "You sure are the best actor, go ahead and act thennnn." Now where I found cheering them on into oblivion to be a bit much, it changed my perspective. It also made me realize that I don't have to be the loudest in the room, the truth detector, nor the voice of reason. His words play in my head when I find myself faced with a situation that, in my past, I would have had to speak out. His words forced me to grow.

I used to need to make sure that my point was heard because I had been silenced for so long. I had felt trapped and diminished. It became natural for me to play the short game where I would react without thinking. It never placed me ahead, and it didn't change the feeling of entrapment. It was just something that deepened my lack of sense of self.

One thing I learned is that no matter how loud you yell, some people will never hear you. I spent many days forcing my point. I needed to get the opportunity to say what I needed to say. I assumed that if the other person heard my side, that they would see my position. Never once did I need the last word. But I did need to say what was on my mind. In any situation where I was robbed of getting my point across, I felt played. You know the feeling that someone got the best of you or someone has the upper hand? That feeling of being handled sucks! No one wants to lose in a situation that should've been a landslide win. Well, that's at least how I felt.

I realized that the only reason I needed to be heard or that I felt played is because I needed to be acknowledged. I needed to be the person who told someone that they were the real wrongdoer. Ultimately, after years of being put down, I always needed to be in the position of winding up on top. It was a sick obsession with no actual reward.

I was in the middle of two situations during law school that didn't end in my favor. Even when my intentions were pure, I ended up isolated, image tainted, and deemed a shit-starter. So how did I find myself there? Well, your girl just had to be heard or try and justify her side. I also was extremely mouthy. I used to make jokes that held a lot of truth but weren't funny in real life. It was in those two moments that being the layer of truth was for the birds. Sometimes speaking the truth comes off like you are messy. It's a fine line to ride, and hell, I straddled it.

I found myself in similar situations when it comes to my family. My family loves a little secret, and I don't do well with secrets. That's too heavy to be holding on to stuff that isn't even deep. But what isn't deep to me was deep to others. Once again, I was straddling that fine line and extremely annoyed with it all. People just need to be real in these streets because I can't keep uppp.

Although I would love for people to keep it real, I noticed that I accomplished more when I began to let others win. I reached higher levels of success when I stopped talking so much and lowered my voice in the room. In silence, I was able to learn how to listen effectively. I gained perspective and was able to find solutions to most problems because I saw each situation through several sets of eyes. With this newfound realization, I now can be proactive and reactive all at once. My moves are now naturally ten steps ahead. It may scare some and come off as calculated. But being calculated can be positive in life. For me, it allows me to control my feelings, determine my next move, and filter my reactions. This gave me the power to choose when I wanted to take the back seat. I will be very clear the choice to be in the back seat doesn't constitute another person's freedom to take the front seat without my input or direction. It simply means that I don't need to lead every time, I pick my battles, and some things just don't require all of my energy.

So here's the lesson. My presence will be felt whether I speak or not. I don't need to talk loud for others to hear me. I would much rather be felt than heard. It is okay to let other people win. It is okay to let people shine even if we both know they are boosting. Who am I to stop them from being great? It is not my place to speak someone's truth. If they want people to know the truth, they will say it. I learned that secrets are stupid. But even though I find them stupid, it is not for me to determine whether or not to share that information.

Further, I learned that if a person doesn't give you room to be heard, nine times out of ten it means, they aren't going to receive or listen to you anyway. Don't waste your time. If you know in your heart that you are right or that you could have clarified a situation but aren't given a chance to do so, just take the L and let that person win. Trust me, winning means more to them than losing means to you. People who always need to succeed are suffering from a complex, so there is no need to frustrate yourself to dismantle their issues.

Last but not least, in those moments that you let someone make it or let them win, recognize your growth. Recognize that you no longer are at a place where you desire the need to be acknowledged. Finally, realize that you severed another tie to your soul. And that my friend is a WIN all by itself.

Reclaiming My Time

All of my soul ties have one huge similarity. That similarity is that each one was attached to something outside of myself. Another person or thing controlled each tie. This meant that I had no control over my well-being. Don't get it twisted; I put up a fight. The problem wasn't that I hadn't tried to fight. The problem was that I didn't know the depth of my opponent. I wasn't equipped to defeat it. To be super real with ya'll, I don't understand why the moments that transpired from the end of November 2019 through the middle of January 2020 created a mental shift so strong that it severed every tie surrounding my soul, but I am not complaining, not one bit. During that time frame, I realized that I would never be enough for many, never have the ability to make others proud and that those people will never recognize the turmoil they brought to my life. They didn't know that through their anguish, they had placed an enormous amount of pain on my shoulders, of which I had no strength to remove. Yet, through that realization, I began seeing myself through new eyes. I recognized the reasons behind the walls that were placed in front of me. And the most significant piece of it all was that I found the strength to knock those walls down.

So, what transpired that was so monumental to wake me up and sever my ties? Well, remember in the beginning when I spoke about my mom telling my husband that she didn't like who I had become and that I was a bad mother? That was the start of an entire shit show. But what really solidified the shift was when my husband asked me for a divorce. He and I had an argument. This disagreement was not huge, but it went left because too much of my dismay, I inherited some of my mom's characteristics that reveal themselves at the worst times possible. Anyway, during this argument, I used a tactic that my mom used all too often. One that my husband saw as a method of manipulation and a red flag. I told ya'll that my husband is a very strong-willed person. He made it clear that he wouldn't be married to a woman that behaved like my mother because my mom repeatedly gets out of pocket. While he knew in his head, he didn't want to be without his family, he was scared that the depth of this hold that my mom had over me had no end. He always said that I only react or recognize things when it gets extreme. He figured a divorce was as radical as it gets.

Hear me and hear me well. I was sooooooooooo angry and hurt! There I was at 29 with two kids, a temporary well-paying political job (emphasis on temporary), staying at my narcissist mom's house, and riding around in a raggedy car. This dude tried my entire life. So, you're just gonna make me a baby mama after we agreed that this was forever?! I was so mad at myself for not being able to see the damage that was caused throughout the years. Why hadn't I been able to move around? I was so angry that I was now in a position to lose my family. I was about to lose the ability to be with the man who was meant for me. I know there is a saying about letting someone go, and if they come back, then it is meant to be. Look, I didn't have time to test that theory, and I deal with facts, not hypotheses.

On top of the anger, I was hurt at the thought that he would leave me in a time when I already was close to breaking free. I was hurt because I wanted him to stay along for the ride, even if I never came to a revelation. Hell, he had been doing it all this time why the sudden change of heart?

But that's just it. He had watched me and been there through it all. He hated seeing me be stuck, hated seeing me drown. I was wrong for finding comfort in the thought that he would always be there. I was wrong for expecting him not to find a breaking point. I was hurt because I was busy trying to find a way to make him forget how fucked up it all was, instead of finding the reason why it was fucked up in the first place.

Clearly, you know that I am still married. So how did I change his mind? Well, I didn't change his mind. This fool knew all along he wasn't going anywhere. He calls it his 'scared straight attempt.' If I were violent, I would've smacked him, but I don't roll like that. But I am weirdly grateful that he did what he did. You see, I was already on the road towards a breakthrough, but his little stunt fast-tracked it.

Now that you know the "big moment," you have a better view as to why I said that I couldn't give you steps. All I know is that this moment opened my eyes, allowing me to dismantle my mental barriers and find the roots of it all.

I am so glad I finally made it to this point, so now it is time to take a page out of Congresswoman Maxine Waters's book and start RECLAIMING MY TIMEEEEEEE!!!

The audacity of all that had control over me. Let me get that back, playaaaaa.

It is one thing to lose control right before your eyes. But to be robbed of control before you could truly spell the word control is a whole different situation. I will never be able to go back and get the time I lost. I will never be able to experience my childhood through childlike eyes. I will never be able to undo the failed relationships I experienced, nor will I be able to give the old me purpose. That's not a possibility.

But what is possible is a total rebuild. I have the capability to never lose control again. I have the ability to choose who has access to the mind, heart, time, and presence. I'm able to build myself up and fuel my self-worth. I now know I don't have to doubt my abilities and I am armed to step into my purpose. I place a return to sender on everything that I lost, and I expect it back in my possession effective immediately.

The funny part about reclaiming control is the people or things that once held the strings can't seem to understand the newfound sense of self. They are so caught off guard by the new and improved person that is before them. They become angry that you are aware of the power you possess and that they no longer have a hand on how you move. It scares them. They start having a case of amnesia. They become the victim and want to know why you are acting this way.

They start telling you that you are acting too cocky and need to humble yourself. Suddenly, you have made them the very outsider that they had once made you. It is not intentional by any means. It just comes with the territory.

No one regains control to punish others. Regaining control is meant for the person who lost it. So why would a thief of power feel like it is a personal vendetta towards them? Clearly, some part of them knows they were wrong. They may or may not acknowledge their wrongdoings, but trust me, they know what they did. The biggest piece I had to remember while I gathered my life, was that if given a chance to continue doing what they had done, they would. I had no room to let up. I needed to own every inch of my life. If I left any room for someone to take control, best believe they will take it.

Too many times, I've been counted out by those who didn't deserve to sit in the same room with me. So, I'm going to be frank when I direct this to those individuals, "You don't compete where you don't compare." Now that you know your place and if you ever find yourself feeling froggy enough to leap at the chance to tear me down, remember it's Dr. Drummond to you. And in the famous words of Birdman, go ahead and put some RESPECT on my name.

But I hope they learned a lesson from it all. I hope they learned that they better be careful because it's all fun and games until someone pulls a you on you.

I'll let that sink in.

And in the meantime, I'll bask in the feeling I have in knowing that I made it to this moment and that I made Auntie Maxine proud.

Time has been SUCCESSFULLY reclaimed.

Chapter 7

A Moment Like This

*"Remember the things you thought you couldn't live without.
Well look at you living and shit."*

Mood

Moment Like This - Kelly Clarkson
Moment 4 Life - Nicki Minaj

So here I am approaching thirty and finally breaking free. In the beginning, I was frustrated and ashamed that it took so long for me to recognize the hold that was over me. Even more so, I was angry that I had been weak. It didn't dawn on me that I was only a child when it all began. I was unable to give myself credit that despite the length of the journey, I was truly fortunate that I caught it before worse things happened. I caught it before it had a trickle effect on my children. I caught it before any thought of harming myself could invade my mind. Reality is that as bad as things were for me, they could've been a thousand times worse.

At this moment, I am no longer concerned with the amount of time that has passed. I don't know if it was a coincidence or just the path designed for me, but from the moment that I broke free, my life has never been the same. My career has taken off, and I now have opened new revenue streams that I likely wouldn't have pursued. My marriage is so much better. My husband and I enjoy each other now more than ever. Although I am now extremely busy with work, I enjoy every moment I get to spend with my kids. Watching them develop and grow is the best part of my existence.

To think that I could have missed this moment. Man, I can't even imagine that. I am so blessed to be here right now, writing this book, sharing some of my vulnerable thoughts. This was not easy. Not by a long shot. But boy does it feel good to be on this side of the tracks.

From this day forward, I vow to maintain control. I vow to be the best wife and mother possible. I vow never to let anyone tear me down to build themself up. I vow to step into my purpose with grace and poise. I vow to explore new possibilities and not allow my old habits to affect any future endeavors. More importantly, I vow to unapologetically be the best version of myself.

It was emotionally taxing to reduce my years of trauma down to fit into this book because, believe me, if I gave you detail by detail, this would be as long as the Harry Potter series. Also, this isn't a tell-all book. I didn't write this to make anyone feel the pain they caused or force them to reflect. I wrote this book in the way that best described the moment. I didn't seek to soften my experiences or how it would make others feel. I wrote this book as a goodbye to my pain and the commencement of the woman I have become. I am sure that this won't sit well with some, and they may choose to never speak to me again. I anticipated that, yet here we are and the book is done. You see, when you are truly past the trauma, you don't fear the outcome of speaking on things that held you down. I am not a hostage to familial norms, expectations, or traditions. I didn't need permission, nor did I feel the need to prepare an explanation. Quite frankly, I don't give a shit how anyone receives this message, because it was never about them. This book is for me. With each chapter, I said, fuck you and goodbye to the pain. It felt so good. I won't ever in this lifetime or the next, apologize for the relief I now feel. I deserve to spend the rest of my days in pure bliss, and that's exactly what I intend to do.

At the beginning of this journey, I am certain you didn't know of my existence, let alone know my name. Hopefully, at this point, you know a little bit of both. I appreciate you getting on this ride and experiencing all the ups and downs that came with it. While I know, I didn't give you a step by step process to help you reach your moment of awakening. I do believe I shared with you the process that took place in my mind, the process that severed the ties of my soul, the process that led me right to this very page. This book is a conversation that I had with myself in real-time. Each chapter was me unveiling the truths of the wounds that held me down for so long. Sometimes new truths emerged as I typed. Sometimes they shocked me, and sometimes they made me cry. But overall, those truths are exactly what they are my truth, and no one can take that away from me. I sit here incredibly proud of how far I've come. I sit satisfied with the thought that I don't live in the shadows of my pain. Much like adulting, darkness is the ghetto, and I don't like it there. But I now know what it looks like, and I can recognize the majority of the signs. If I see it's ghetto ass trying to creep back into existence, I will be prepared, fist up, ready to knock it right out of my life.

At some point, I know I will be asked to put this book into a category, but I am not sure there is one that does this justice. I am making one up. Let's call it a "Sit Down Series" or a "How I" instead of a "How To". That's the best way to describe it. I truly believe that no self-help book would've gotten me here. So many people experience soul ties in all kinds of forms. I find it hard to believe that there is an article, book, or blog post that advises to rid a person of all forms all at once. I would bet my last dollar on it. Now listen, if you so happen to find something that addresses every soul tie imaginable, don't come checking for my dollar. But seriously, there aren't many words of wisdom out there that can truly divest you of all the toxic inhabitants of your soul. For me, it all led up to a scared straight moment. For you, it could be the opportunity to yell on a mountain top. Regardless of how you get to the land of the free, it is crucial to remember it isn't about what we do once we reach the top, it's imperative to acknowledge the journey of the climb.

I keep trying to find words to drag this out so that our journey together doesn't come to an end, but I have absolutely nothing left to say. This is shocking because I could talk the ear off of a tree if you let me. But I have to say goodbye. I genuinely hope you enjoyed our time together. Who knows, maybe one day we'll find ourselves on another ride for another adventure of my life, hell it may be a ride about your experience. Either way, I look forward to the possibility to journey together again.

It has truly been my pleasure. So, until we meet again, I wish you nothing but the best!

Warm Regards,

Yladrea N. Drummond, J.D.

Acknowledgments

To God - I thank you because you kept me in the midst of it all.

To my loving husband, Kendrick – Thank you for safeguarding my heart and for all the sacrifices you made to give me room to grow and pursue my dreams.

To my two amazing little boys, Karson and Kannon – Thank you for giving me a thousand reasons to keep going even when I didn't think I had the strength.

To my wonderful friends – Thank you for sticking around even though I know it wasn't easy.

About the Author

Yladrea is a native of Houston, Texas. She is an accomplished compliance consultant, lawyer, political strategist, and leadership trainer. She holds a B.A. in Political Science from Texas State University and a Juris Doctor from Southern University Law Center. Yladrea is the Founder & CEO of Capital Strategies, LLC, which is the first black-owned political/NGO compliance and financial services firm in the United States. Additionally, she is the Founder of The Ink Up, an organization dedicated to expanding the power of black literature and those behind the pen. Above all of her accomplishments, she takes pride in her biggest role as a wife and mother of her two sons. When it's all said and done, Yladrea pledges her life's mission, to uplift others, be a vessel for the unheard, and tackle injustice across the nation.

Made in the USA
Columbia, SC
10 December 2020